Pagan Planet

Being, Believing & Belonging in the 21st Century

Pagan Planet

Being, Believing & Belonging in the 21st Century

Edited by Nimue Brown

MOON BOOKS

Winchester, UK
Washington, USA

First published by Moon Books, 2016
Moon Books is an imprint of John Hunt Publishing Ltd., Laurel House, Station Approach,
Alresford, Hants, SO24 9JH, UK
office1@jhpbooks.net
www.johnhuntpublishing.com
www.moon-books.net

For distributor details and how to order please visit the 'Ordering' section on our website.

ISBN: 978 1 78279 783 8
Library of Congress Control Number: 2015939704

A CIP catalogue record for this book is available from the British Library.

Design: Stuart Davies

Printed and bound by CPI Group (UK) Ltd, Croydon, CR0 4YY, UK

CONTENTS

Foreword

By Mike Stygal, President of the Pagan Federation

So I was asked if I might write a little as a foreword to the book you hold in your hands. Why me? I wondered, and still wonder to a certain extent. But then, thinking further, I realise that this is but another extension of my service to the Pagan community, and indeed, the wider community. I feel extremely honoured to have been given the opportunity to comment upon a work that collates some of the thoughts of 46 different Pagan authors, each reflecting on aspects of Paganism in the world today and each in their own unique and creative way.

Paganism encompasses a great deal of diversity, from the numerous Pagan traditions followed and the diversity within those traditions themselves through to the very individual way our experiences of living on this planet influence our understanding, interpretation and manifestation of our traditions. To some, the extent of the diversity within Paganism is viewed as a negative challenge. How can Pagans have any kind of unity if they're so very different from one another? Surely any attempt to find unity would be akin to herding cats? My own perspective on that is a little complicated. But it begins from the premise that we live in an extremely diverse society, and within that society there are many points upon which people with diverse backgrounds can find unity. It begins from the recognition that we all share a common uniting factor in that we are all humans living on the same planet. This is actually very much the same approach I take to working with people from other faith traditions and it is my belief that the great diversity we find within Paganism, and the experience of working with that diversity, lends itself to the development of the necessary skills required for effective interfaith dialogue. I remember one encounter at an interfaith gathering where a faith representative (identification concealed to protect the temporarily ill informed) was adamant that there really was no place for including Pagans in interfaith as we were all godless and had nothing to connect us to the faiths represented in the group. In beginning from a perspective of fellow humans dwelling on the same planet, within the same wider community, and working up from there to inform the misinformed, that rejecting opinion was not sustained. But I digress. I have often heard Paganism described as a collection of earth-venerating traditions. I firmly believe that such a description has some merit. But it doesn't quite capture a full description of Pagan traditions. My standard description would be something along the lines of:

> Paganism is a collection of spiritual or religious paths that are largely rooted in indigenous traditions – mainly from Europe, and many of which could be said to focus on a reverence for nature.

Long winded and still not as inclusive as it could be, but possibly hinting a little more closely towards a way Paganism might find unity within its diversity. One of the things you might begin to glimpse as you work through this anthology is the threads of concepts that could begin to unite a great many Pagans.

I first began consciously identifying as Pagan in 1986. Over the intervening years I have explored ceremonial magick, Druidry, Anglo-Saxon magic, Shamanism, Wicca and traditional witchcraft. Each step along the path has provided information and foundations for the path I now follow, which might be described as using Shamanic techniques to explore a relationship with the British landscape. Labels, I find, have their uses as a basic indicator, but require much more information to be supplied in order to gain a more accurate picture. Even then, our own understanding of language used can colour our understanding of the spiritual experiences and practices of another.

I've been a volunteer with the Pagan Federation, in one role or another, for about a decade now. One of the aims of the Pagan Federation is to seek to support all Pagans in their personal and public life, to help ensure that they have the same rights as the followers of other beliefs and members of other religions. In order to do that, it is important to consider Pagans as a part of wider society and to go further in considering what role Pagans might have to play within that wider society. As people, of course, Pagans might play an extremely varied role within society. But identifying particularly Pagan ways that Pagans might play a role in society might be a little more difficult, particularly because of our diversity. Again, it is my feeling that, as you read through this anthology, you might begin to glimpse some ways in which Pagans might make a particularly Pagan contribution to society.

I sincerely hope you enjoy this anthology, and that it prompts much thought and even more understanding of the modern Pagan experience in the 21st century. So without further ado, I commend you to the *real* experts. Happy reading.

Introduction

By Nimue Brown

Contributors to this anthology were drawn from the lively pool of Moon Books authors, from the wider Moon Books community and then, as the book progressed, from a little further afield. The subtitle: *Being, Believing & Belonging in the 21st Century* rapidly took on a life of its own, offering as it does a challenge to say how we're handling what are difficult and perhaps defining times for our species and the world we inhabit.

As so many contributors spoke of activism, it made increasing sense to reach out to known activists who are not habitual writers to get their voices and experiences into the mix. There are many stories here that need to be heard, not least because these are tales of regular people hearing a call and working out what to do with that, from projects on the global scale to determined acts at the hearth. Voices combine to create a sense of momentum and of possibility.

If we want a place to be and to belong, we have to take better care of the planet. Belief and pragmatism draw closer all the time. Nature is sacred to us, and nature is life.

Rich gold of sunset on my brow,
Silver flash of a thousand lapwings.
For the mint, I find it wild
In watery coombes and valleys.
Gem bright insects in profusion,
While my banks show primrose
Bramble and wild dog rose.
I have invested in seeds,
Planting trees towards the future,
And my hedge is a foraging fund

Of sloe, elderberries, mushrooms.
Growth in grass is good just now;
Bulls and bears in their own meadows.
My stocks, night scented beauties.
The trickle down of rainwater,
For all my wealth is life.

PaganAid and the Road to Social Justice

By Ian Chandler, Founder of PaganAid

The first seed that led to my setting up PaganAid was sown more than 20 years ago when I visited an agricultural training centre in Zimbabwe. On the way, I had driven with some Oxfam colleagues down a long road where the contrast between the two sides could not have been more extreme. On the right, behind the high wire fence, rainbows sparkled as the array of sprinklers pumped countless gallons of water through the hot African sun, drenching the vast fields of vivid green maize as they reached for the sky. On the other side of the road, the unfenced fields stretched flat and grey as the millet and sorghum plants cried out with thirst while all around the earth turned to desert. Same soil, same climate, but two different worlds. But what both sides of the road had in common was that neither were sustainable – they both destroyed the local environment and made people poorer. The big industrial farm depended on sucking up all the available water from the surrounding region and mixed it with tanker loads of fertilisers, insecticides and herbicides. On the other side, poor farmers tending their small plots were unable to afford irrigation, but were still being encouraged to adopt 'modern' European farming practices and plant high-yield (but high-risk) seeds that relied on plentiful water and chemical fertilisers, which they bought with borrowed money. Rarely were they able to grow and sell enough crops to get themselves out of debt and improve their farms and lives.

The training centre was radically different. Crops were growing confidently in the shade of trees, mulched with natural compost to keep the moisture in the ground and improve the soil, planted alongside flowers that repelled pests. There were no sprinklers and no chemicals either. Instead of fighting it, farmers were learning to live in harmony with nature. In Europe, we would call this permaculture. In Africa, it was simply described as rediscovering traditional farming techniques appropriate for arid lands.

I was deeply committed to fighting poverty and promoting human rights, but I also wanted to protect and preserve the environment. These two goals often seemed to be in conflict. Mainstream thinking on poverty reduction was founded on a model of economic growth, increased production and increased consumption. This project demonstrated that another way is possible, recognising that as poverty and environmental destruction are two sides of the same coin, to solve one, we need to solve both. The project did not have all the answers – poverty is much more than hunger and low incomes – but it was a window onto a different form of development.

Since then, I have been fortunate enough to see many other projects that link the relief of extreme poverty with promoting human rights and protecting the environment.

In Vietnam, I have visited schools that had set up their own tree nurseries to teach their pupils about forestry and environmental protection. They also helped fund teachers' salaries by selling young trees to the local community. I have seen mangrove forests planted on the water's edge that hold back the sea when the typhoons rage, protecting the people and their crops from devastating flash floods.

In Brazil, I have met the widows of tribal leaders who were killed while defending their communal lands from forestry and mining companies, and who still continue the fight to preserve their people's lifestyle and dignity. I have met families who for years had been living under plastic sheeting on the streets of São Paulo before grouping together to invade and occupy massive abandoned haciendas (commercial farms and plantations) owned by rich landowners, risking the bullets of the hired gunman who tried to drive them off. Working together, they built timber homes and schools, divided up the fields, planted hedges and trees, and grew their food in a sustainable manner.

In the 30 years that I have been working to combat poverty and help poor and marginalised communities to claim their voice, huge strides have been made. The number of people living in extreme poverty has more than halved. However, the injustices in today's world are still rampant. As Mahatma Ghandi rightly said: '*The world has enough for everyone's need, but not enough for everyone's greed.*' The industrialised world's addiction to growth at all costs, its craving to rip out and consume all the precious gifts of Mother Nature, is destroying the world we live in. The air and water are being poisoned. The land is being stripped of its trees and natural vegetation, the earth raped for its minerals. Countless species are being murdered to extinction, never to return. And many of the human children of Mother Earth and Father Sky are being driven deeper into poverty and suffering.

If someone has more than they need, and someone else does not have enough to feed their children, then where is the justice? And, as it is the rich who set the rules, is it any wonder that there is conflict? When just 85 billionaires have more wealth than the poorest half of the world's population combined, their ability to influence governments and capture the political process can go unchallenged. The radical Brazilian educator Paulo Freire wrote: '*Washing one's hands of the conflict between the powerful and the powerless means to side with the powerful, not to be neutral.*' I believe that to be a true Pagan, to live our lives with love and integrity, we cannot be neutral in the face of extreme poverty and environmental destruction; we have to stand up for what we believe in.

It is claimed that the ancient Druids were peacemakers, and we often call for peace in our rituals. But what does it mean to be a peacemaker? Peace is not passivity – peace is active. Peace does not mean the absence of warfare – peace means harmony. And peace can only come where there is justice. If there is no justice, then discontent festers, harmony breaks down and conflict erupts. In order to be peacemakers, the Druid priests of old were the judges, solving grievances and helping communities to understand their interdependence with each other and with nature. They were the advisors to the chiefs, encouraging them to respect the gods and spirits of the place, and rule in the long-term interests of the whole community, not just for their own immediate self-interest.

My Druidry is rooted in a commitment to social and environmental justice. I believe in honouring our ancestors, being inspired by their example, but also learning from their mistakes. I believe that all of Mother Earth's creations have an inherent value and beauty, equally deserving of our love and respect. Humanity as a species has been responsible for destruction on a massive scale, but individuals are not equally to blame or worthy of punishment. My love extends beyond the rivers and the mountains, and the flora and fauna of the natural world, to include those struggling to survive, fighting to feed their children and longing to live with dignity and security.

I also believe that to be a Druid is to be committed to service – service to the natural world and service to our human world. As the planet shrinks through faster transport and communications, that human world extends beyond our own immediate communities to all of our brothers and sisters across the globe. It is this belief in service that has driven me to work in international development for more than three decades, and ultimately led me to set up a charity for Pagans to act in solidarity with the world's poor and support sustainable development.

It had a long gestation.

As a committed Pagan working in development for both secular and faith-based charities (such as Christian Aid and CAFOD), I often bemoaned the lack of a truly Pagan charity committed to ending poverty and protecting the environment. Every time I asked: 'Why doesn't *someone* set one up for Pagans?' I knew in my heart that the question was aimed at me, but I resisted the call for years.

Indeed, there were plenty of good reasons not to do it. Setting up a new aid charity would be a lot of unpaid hard work. There are worthwhile secular charities around that Pagans can donate to if they don't want to support a Christian, Muslim or Jewish one. Coming out as a Pagan in the charity sector might damage the income I earn as a freelance consultant.

I was also worried about whether anybody in the Pagan community would be interested. As I talked to more people, however, I realised that the majority of Pagans are deeply committed to social and environmental justice – locally and globally. Many are engaged in political debate and campaigning. Many more volunteer their time or give regularly to various charities. They recognise that we live on one planet and that our future is tied up inextricably with the fate of everyone else. If their boat sinks, so does ours. But more than this, they want to move beyond self-interest and be connected to others as part of something larger. They want a charity that they can identify with as Pagans and call their own, a trusted means by which they can support people to defend their rights and work their way out of extreme poverty, living with dignity and in harmony with nature, protecting the environment that we all share.

I also wanted the Pagan community to have an opportunity to talk openly about our values and our radical vision for the future, rather than just our beliefs and ritual practices, which tends to be the majority of the (mostly negative) media coverage and public discourse on Paganism. If we had our own aid charity, this could be seen as a sign that Paganism had matured, that we don't need to be defensive, but can hold our heads up with pride in what we are achieving across the globe.

Ultimately, I could no longer resist the call and started to take practical steps to set up PaganAid. I talked to many leading figures in the Pagan community who offered their enthusiastic support. Greywolf (Chief of the British Druid Order) and Mike

Stygal (President of the Pagan Federation) agreed to join our small board of trustees. We wrote a constitution that set out our objectives to support sustainable development through funding appropriate projects in poor countries. We would promote an alternative model of development that was not based on economic growth and acquiring more material goods, but was about happiness and dignity – having enough to meet basic needs, but also living in peace and harmony with nature. As we got established, we would also campaign to encourage those with more than enough to live simply so that others could simply live and Mother Earth could breathe more easily.

We then submitted an application to the Charity Commission of England and Wales to be registered as a charity. How would the Charity Commission react to our proposal? Would they accept our goals as charitable? How would our Paganism affect our application? Would we get official recognition? Finally, we received our answer: yes, our application had been approved and we were an officially registered charity! There was no turning back now, and the real work began of setting up bank accounts and websites, writing publicity materials and planning our launch.

PaganAid may only be a small charity at the moment, but mighty oaks grow from little acorns. If Pagans around the world plant seeds of hope by supporting PaganAid, then together those seeds will grow a forest of fairness, where people live with dignity and in harmony with nature.

I have been working to fight poverty, promote human rights and protect the environment for more than 30 years. In that time, I have heard people's stories that have made me cry, I have seen destruction that has brought me to my knees with despair. But I have also met people whose dedication against all odds fills me with awe. I have seen achievements that make me want to sing and dance in the street. Now is not the time for us to give up on the future – it is time for us to decide what future we want, and to make that future happen.

To find out more about PaganAid or to make a donation, please visit www.paganaid.org

Castle Hill, Penwortham: An Alternative Story

By Lorna Smithers

Castle Hill in Penwortham is a magical place, in spite of the damage. Obscured by the bypass, partly built on by a housing estate, its holy wells dried up and covered over and its priory destroyed, St Mary's Church, its leaning gravestones and the motte are the only recognised features that remain.

However, spend a little time walking its old paths and woodlands, seeing beyond the Christian nomenclature and usurped seat of Norman rule, and another world opens. A world within and without the hollow hill; a world of wild fairies shut out and ignored, ghosts of water spirits who sang at the wells, a dragon power lost beneath.

Castle Hill's religious and military significance is well documented by historians. The effects of the predominance of Christianity, industrialisation and development on the spirits of place have not been explored. This is an alternative story, passed on by its spirits, by decree of the fay king.

The Alternative Story of Castle Hill

At the heart of the hill lay a water dragon. She awoke at the end of the Ice Age when the land began to thaw. From her giving womb burst myriad springs, carving gullies where mosses and ferns sprang.

At the hill's foot a thirsty auroch was the first creature to drink from the purest, most powerful spring, which flowed into a natural pool. The rest of the herd followed, then red deer, wild horses and the first hunter gatherers who built their nearby lake village beside the river of shining water.

These early people venerated the spring. Listening to its ever-pouring stream, behind it many heard the song of the dragon's daughter. It was rumoured she could be seen by moonlight. She first appeared as a pale woman, but look again and you would see her scales and glimmering tail. To this strange spirit the people attributed the spring's healing powers.

A line of Brythonic women presided over the spring, serving its spirit, meting its cures until their last representative was slaughtered by the Romans. This tradition remained in the memory of the local people. Therefore when the missionaries arrived they moved quickly in rededicating the spring to St Mary. A stone basin was built and a stone cross erected over the new well, inscribed with the Magnificat.

Over the years it became a site of pilgrimage. Strangers travelled from across the country to marvel at its picturesque glade at the hill's foot, overlooked by a canopy of beech, surrounded by ivy and primroses. Although forbidden, the healing rituals continued, evidenced by multicoloured floating ribbons. People immersed themselves in its waters, took their horses in with them. It was finally decided these activities must stop and the well was capped.

Throughout this time the dragon's daughter was ignored, yet she still gave, even though her spring was forced irreverently into a trickling metal pipe. Then something catastrophic happened.

The river was moved southward to make way for the docklands. The sandstone beneath the hill sealing the aquifer was breached. Down below the water dragon experienced an inexplicable pain. Writhing, gasping within the chasm, her womb imploded. Her features shrunk and fell inward, becoming sheer water sucked away through the shattered bedrock. The being of her daughters unravelled with her, shrieking backward into disappearance.

St Mary's well ran dry. Local people were deprived of their cleanest source of water. Prevalent whispers spoke of the bad omen, yet the fault of the developers was not revealed. There was nothing to worry about; piped water would be coming soon, for a hefty fee. The well was buried, out of sight and out of mind.

Yet it remains on old maps and in the memory of the land, which does not forget; in a cold, empty cavern and tunnels where streams ran but are no more. At the spring's old site or wandering the hill at certain liminal times, you might sense a dragon's heartbeat or hear her final gasp. You may glimpse the ghosts of her daughters, hear their last screams.

When winter's king ruled over the Ice Age, driving glaciers over the land to carve its new shape with blizzard snows and harsh winds, he and his spirits paused to rest at this hollow hill, which they entered to feast, dance and make merry. Wondering at its illumined caverns and the intricate beauty of its slowly forming water dragon some of them begged to stay.

His task near complete, knowing it would soon be time to retreat to the underworld, winter's king agreed. He assigned these spirits the role of protecting the hill and its water dragon, told them they must teach its people of the ways between the worlds and take them into its halls upon their death. Every winter they must ensure the path to the underworld remained open for his hunt.

When the hill thawed, the spirits mixed with the first trees; a surrounding scrubby tundra of birch replaced with huge bog oaks thick with mosses. The first people to venture into these groves sensed their presence in the unwarranted snap of twigs and warning cries of crows, heard their piping tunes and mournful refrains. However, only certain people could see and communicate with them.

To these Brythonic seers they appeared in many guises. Sometimes they took the face of the woodland clad in bark and leaf. At others they appeared near human, as tall beings of bright, unbearable beauty, or hooded, hunched and withered, crumbling into decay and death. Frequently they took the apparel of ancestors, living friends and relatives.

As promised, they taught the early people to lead their funeral processions along the spirit path, to erect a mound on the summit of the hill and to bury their dead with weapons, coins, flagons and cutlery for use in the afterlife. They were invoked to guide the dead into the hill and in return gifted with spiralling incense, spiced cake and mead.

The Britons only visited the hill on select occasions; for funerals and seasonal rites where the worlds met for feasting and dancing. Most times it was set aside for the spirits and through the coldest months it was abandoned entirely for the passage of the hunt.

These traditions were maintained until the missionaries came. Horrified by the prevailing beliefs they dismantled the burial mound and reburied the bones in the Christian way. In its place a wooden church was erected and was dedicated to St Mary, who was to replace the female seers who communed with the underworld. During its consecration solemn chanting and lashings of holy water ensured the 'evil' spirits were kept at bay.

Cut off from the summit and their role in guiding the dead, some spirits retreated into the hill. Others vented their anger in raging winds, storming through the woodlands, felling trees. As the people turned their veneration from the hill to invisible deities of heaven it was subsumed in endless rain, unremitting damp and swirling shadows.

By the time the Normans seized rule and built their motte, castle and priory, Peneverdant, 'the green hill on the water' was renowned for being an unpleasant, god-forsaken place. The monks sent from Evesham were as drunk and disreputable as they could get. Of course, they blamed it on the weather. They dared not mention the strange laughter, irresistible lures, dark threats and paralysing fear that gripped them on winter nights as something cold and fathomless swept by, lifting them from their beds. Once the castle had served its purpose the rulers were swift to depart from the hill, leaving the timber structure to ruin and decay.

Over the years the surrounding landscape was tamed, drained and parcelled out as meadows and pasture. As the village of Penwortham grew, St Mary's Church was rebuilt in stone and its graveyard consecrated. Remembering the devilish spirits and their lust for the souls of the deceased, the priests ensured loud bells were rung to ward them off at every funeral.

However, this did not prevent their portents. In the 19th century two men saw a procession of black-clad fairies in red caps carrying a coffin on Church Avenue. One of the men looked into the coffin, saw his own corpse and died shortly afterward.

Irreparable change came to the 'fairies' when the water dragon disappeared. Unable to fathom how and why the tools of mankind brought about the demise of the giving creature they had loved and served for centuries, some longed to throw themselves down the chasm after her. Others entered an intense state of mourning and remain catatonic to this day. Unrepeatable curses on mankind rang around the empty cavern and echoed throughout Lancashire in the wind and rain.

Eventually their king arrived. Grave farewells to the water dragon and her daughters were made within and at the sites of the springs. There has been no feasting or dancing in the hill since.

Shortly afterward the woodland beside Church Avenue was cut down to make way for expensive properties, tarmacked and given over to the motor car. The spirit path ruined, the fairies were forced to move their route from the hill's summit to a dirt trackway at its foot running through Penwortham Wood.

In the healing arms of the lady of the wood they settled slowly and came to love the last fragment of their magical landscape. Their whispers encouraged sycamore and ash to bend into a natural archway, heavy ivy to climb and hang like chandeliers, dripping mosses to adorn hawthorn and elder. The chorus of blackbird, robin and wren encouraged them to sing. Their procession was seen again and the trackway became known as Fairy Lane.

Looking north to the nearby river they noticed the dark swell of industrial pollution had ceased. In the clear waters salmon and trout re-emerged. Herons and cormorants came to join the flocks of gulls. The birds told them upriver an otter had been seen nursing her cubs in the rushes. In this they recognised the guiding hand of its goddess, Belisama.

However, their sorrows had not ended. Spewing noise and pollution from its twin concrete viaducts as it roared over the river, Penwortham Bypass was built, casting the woodland into unnatural shade. The view of the hill was obscured for good. Restless and embittered, their wrath lingers as rot. Trees fall to the road's vibrations, gravestones topple and dead man's fingers creep from logs. To ward off unwelcome humans they skew their forms into grotesque, malevolent goblins wielding savage spears.

As winter approaches their king appears as Gwyn ap Nudd, a fearsome warrior-huntsman with a blackened face on a dark horse huge as the hill, an infinity of hounds baying behind him. Seeing the precarious state of the hill, its woodland and his spirit path, he perceives its story must be told, before it is too late.

The Impact of Paganism

By Fiona Tinker

The brief was 1,500 words of personal writing. The subject – what's it like being a Pagan in the 21st century? The initial flippant response was: 'Not that much different from being a Pagan in the 20th century,' but, on reflection, that's not quite true.

My Paganism started in my home country, developed in another, matured in yet another and finally returned home with the eventual intention of laying its bones in the land of my birth. Journeying through the years, physically and psychically, taught me much and made for many interesting encounters with wonderful people and places. However, the millennium seemed to have marked a turning point, one between private and public, not just between centuries.

Let me share some stories from the last century.

North Lanark, Scotland

I'm a child, sitting on a log laid across a burn, watching the tadpoles in the water as they nibble at my feet. It's a still day and not a soul is about. I should be in the chapel. It's another boring old Sunday in the days when the world shut down on the Sabbath, but it's easy to walk with the crowd to the door of the chapel then skirt around the building, climb over the back fence and head for the freedom of the fields beyond. I prefer to listen to the land, the wind and the water. And the stories they tell.

I meet people. They're on a yearly cycle of moving through the land. Some are passing through just for a week or so, others stay longer. All of them have stories; about the land, about the Gods and Goddesses and about the people of old. I'm hungry. I eat their stories more readily that I could ever cannibalise the transubstantiated body and blood of the figure I am told I must believe in.

I don't believe in him. I believe in auld Lizzie and her wonderful stories. Her wonderful world of words is there to explore. It feels like it is all mine too and I hug it to myself.

And, as Lizzie told me, the lands tell their stories to those who choose to listen.

Stonehenge Free Festivals, England

A time of optimism and joy. Stories of being young.

Avebury, England

An April weekend and I'm there with someone I love. We're tootling around exploring the south-west in an old van. It's freezing; we've woken early and gone for a walk along the ridges circling the monument just to warm up. It's very early in the morning and a heavy mist lies over everything. I'm in my element; I could be at any point in time, and all that is here is an ancient landscape, two humans and some sheep. My lover is uncomfortable – he doesn't do this 'Pagan stuff' and he's probably watched *The Wicker Man* once too often. Suddenly there comes the sound of low chanting through the mist. I stand stock still, curious, whilst my knight turns a graveyard grey.

The chanting grows louder and footsteps accompany it. It's not English, it's Latin. I'm really curious now, but admittedly a little unnerved too. Through the mist, we can suddenly just make out a crowd of people marching, holding a massive flag aloft and – perched on the top of it – is the shape of an eagle. What *is* this? Someone's filming? Did the Romans have a camp here – have we time-slipped or something?

The chanting becomes louder and insistent, as the banner-carrying crowd emerges through the mist…only to reveal themselves as a church group walking around the ditches of Avebury on Easter Sunday singing the praises of their God. This was an excellent lesson on looking and looking again if there ever there was one!

Tara, Ireland

I'm alone and walking up a side path to Tara, which will bring me out into the Banqueting Hall. It is a beautiful summer's day and the path is canopied by the leaves of the trees. It's really peaceful. Suddenly, I hear horses and the jingling of small bells moving with the beat of their hooves, as if they are fastened onto the reins and keeping time with the animals' movements. I turn around and there is nothing there, only the sound of horses. I pull back to the edges of the path and the horses pass. I feel the motion pass my face, hear their hooves and bells and hear – very distinctly – '*Go raibh maith agat – thank you*'.

I wish my grandmother was still alive. I so want to tell her about this. Despite her devotion to Marianne worship, I know she would believe me. When she and my great-aunt, both elderly ladies at the time, were visiting the Glens of Antrim and wallowing in the peace of the wilds, they too had an aural encounter they couldn't explain as beautiful flute music came from nowhere and no-one they could see. They left in a hurry and it was hard to get them to talk about it, so shaken were they by their experience.

Small experiential stories about interacting with the land from three countries, from three different times in my life; all of which have added to the tapestry of my path – but what do they mean? Experiencing a religion is a personal thing. The stories can be told and accepted or rejected by the listeners as they wish. But the deeper meanings and the learning are personal. Sometimes the sense of the Divine is too much to try to explain to another, silence is better.

This Century

So what of the new millennium? What has changed?

That time was spent in Glastonbury, waiting on the torch-lit procession around the Tor. Paganism had come out of the shadows and people were connecting with each other in a way that had not really been possible before the Internet. Glastonbury had always been a centre of something and now that something was growing, reaching out and calling all who would hear. And in the song of that land was a refrain calling me home.

I returned to a very different Scotland in the 21st century from the one I left in the 20th century.

Public silence about Paganism is not as important as it once was, where automatic suspicion would have been the default position of many if one mentioned to them about being Pagan. The Pagan Federations of each country had worked hard – and continue to do so – for acceptance; dispelling the myths and propaganda that had grown up around us. Druid and other Pagan groups are part of national life in all three nations. Moots are many and various. There is a proliferation of information and books. Paganism is studied at universities.

The Scottish Pagan Federation (SPF) worked hard for the recognition and involvement of Pagans in civic life. Its work complemented equalities legislation in Scotland and Pagans are included in civic life, along with the other small faith groups within the country. Civic advocacy work includes things like consultations and working on Government policies; and involvement with Interfaith Scotland, both through local inter-faith groups and through national projects. Religious Pagan marriage was authorised by the General Registrar's Office (Scotland) in 2004. Many Pagans come here to marry in legal Pagan handfasting/religious marriage ceremonies. Further recent equalities legislation has meant that same-sex couples can have legal religious marriages too and Louise Park, Presiding Officer of The Scottish Pagan Federation, celebrated the first Pagan legal same-sex marriage in Edinburgh, in January, 2015.

Of course, not all Pagans in Scotland are members of the SPF. People are different and joining isn't everyone's cup of tea. Being individual, being true to ourselves, is the strength of knowing who we are as people – people who happen to be Pagan. But the SPF's work has helped ensure that all Pagans are generally part of the mainstream here.

There are many groups and moots within Scotland. The inner life is private, as with any religious group, but some also have a public face that has helped shape Paganism in the 21st century. Open rituals are held by some groups in public spaces. These open rituals show that Paganism as just another facet of religious life and many curious people come away from them with more understanding than that with which they arrived.

This is the Scotland I returned to in the 21st century and the background to my Paganism as lived, whether it is in the silence of personal devotion or the more public civic roles I'm involved with.

I look back to the child-me sitting on a log nearly 45 years ago, playing truant from chapel, hugging to my heart the words and music auld Lizzie shared. If someone told me that this would be the future, I would never have believed it, it would have seemed too far-fetched, no matter how many stories I devoured.

Squirrels on 'Shrooms: Divination in the Deep Woods

By Hearth Moon Rising

It's a reasonably cool day for mid-July and I'm hiking the Hurricane Mountain. Hurricane got its name for obvious reasons, being notorious for dangerous storms with high winds. Once, near the summit, a gust threw me off my feet and pinned me against the rock. Today, however, the wind speaks softly in the fluttering of leaves. Today everything is backwards.

I notice a red squirrel on a white pine above my head. It is unusual to see the red squirrel ahead of his piercing shriek. He chatters, cajoles, threatens, and abuses anyone wandering into his territory. In Norse mythology a red squirrel carries insults from a snake monster to the top branches of the World Tree, where a large eagle returns abusive messages of his own. Anyone who knows the red squirrel understands how well suited he is for this task, for he delights in railing anyone for the most trivial of reasons.

But today the squirrel has nothing to say to me. He doesn't harangue, upbraid, remonstrate, or rebuke. He just sits on his branch, eating something, looking at me. With a guarded eye, to be sure, but still... I puzzle over how to interpret this strange sign, except to surmise that my life must be above reproach.

My Craft mainly involves interpreting signs: understanding the language of animals, water, and trees. I use this information to create offerings to the nature deities, and I build on my relationship with these deities to direct my magic. Feedback from natural sources helps me chart the course of my creative work, and it also alerts me to challenges and possibilities. I have learned to draw conclusions from sketchy data, and to keep conclusions tentative, allowing the questions to flow in my capillaries as I await further signs.

A week later I am crossing the boardwalk on Lake Winnifred, enjoying the dragonflies and the lazy buzzing of cicadas, when I encounter another red squirrel. He sits back on hind legs, chewing on what looks like an apple core. Red squirrels don't usually leave the security of conifers, although the swampy brush probably confers some safety. Again, there is no speech and apparently no alarm. Now I am really confused, because I thought this little critter disparaged humans as a matter of principle. As I walk toward him, he hops toward me; then he turns 360 degrees and scampers underneath the bridge. Though this is strange behaviour for a wild animal, I am not concerned about rabies because I just saw him eating. And what was he eating? On closer inspection it is not an apple core but a mushroom, and a mushroom I don't recall from any of my books on culinary fungi. Now things are beginning to make sense; these squirrels are tripping along the boardwalk.

When I return home, I search my field manuals, because I rely on the experience of others as well as my own observations in understanding signs in nature. I learn that the American red squirrel consumes several dozen types of mushroom and is rather fond of the *Amanita* species, whose best known member is the psychotropic fly agaric. He caches fungi in the crevices of tree branches, where they dry, awaiting future storage. No doubt they will be a comfort on blizzardy days and long winter nights.

One piece of wisdom from my laid-back squirrels is now clear: I need to turn my attention to visions. Some would take this as a sign that a psychedelic journey was called for, but I don't need psychotropics to have visions and other factors argue against this interpretation. This is July, the brief season of intense activity in the north, not normally a time when we are inclined to turn inward. My days are relaxed, and I reserve time for meditation, but current projects do not support an extended period of seclusion. Neither my personal inclination nor the astrological influences compel me toward a vision quest at this time, but I have been preoccupied with visioning in another sense: with Vision as a large idea, conceptualised and wished for, but not manifest.

My vision for some time has been to ground modern witchcraft more completely and more concretely in the natural world, to create a deeper understanding of what it means to have an animistic practice. This is something I have tried to do in my book *Invoking Animal Magic*. Lately I have begun looking at magical connection within nature as an ongoing process rather than a goal, and consequently at how to teach the process of connecting. This is a highly creative endeavour for me and for my students, one that involves profound experimentation. My druggie squirrels are signalling that conditions are ready for the voyage, since psychotropic drug use carries a connotation of experimentation as well as vision. The message is to 'go for it'.

A few days later, I am in the conifers with a small group of priestesses. They are game for the adventure, but grumble a bit about bushwhacking, until I remind them that we need to be unobserved and unmolested to release our creative powers. It doesn't occur to me until later that, since what we are doing is definitely off label, we must go off trail to do it. I have confidence in this group's ability to conduct themselves competently in the woods, and they have confidence in my knowledge of magic. The time is ripe for experimenting, for creating the vision.

I don't carry expectations that an experiment will work well at first, or that it will work at all. That's what makes it an experiment. I'm taken by surprise when the energy for this ritual emerges cleanly, spontaneously, directed without concerted effort. I can't remember when I've felt so relaxed leading a ritual. The thrushes sing in harmony with our voices. The squirrels are silent, dreaming with us. We are with the planet, spiralling through a universe of wondrous possibility.

The Wild Sistas

By Edwina Hodkinson

It was a rainy day in September and I gathered with friends at a retreat in Essex to celebrate the Goddess; Elen of the Ways. Kneeling at her altar in ritual space, I put on my antlered headdress and dedicated myself to becoming her priestess, vowing to protecting the land; her land. In the middle of the ceremony, the antlers fell off my head and wouldn't stay on. I should have realised at that moment that she had plans for me. It was not until a few months later, that I would realise just what they were.

Until then I had only been a keyboard warrior, signing numerous petitions and making my MP earn his money by sending him emails on various earth-based and humanitarian issues. I'd been on a couple of family-friendly protest marches in London and was always keen to be involved in community projects. Any direct action that involved the risk of arrest or conflict with the police had never entered my arena. As a Pagan, following a Goddess path for many years, I have always seen protection of the earth and its inhabitants as an integral part of my spiritual path. I am an outdoorsy kind of woman with a love of wild places, plants and trees. Having the wind in my hair, rain on my skin and mud on my boots on the top of desolate Pennine moorland or woodland is my idea of bliss. Working as a medical herbalist with a passion for local plant medicine was something that came naturally to me and connects me very deeply to the ancestors and the land.

I'd not really given fracking much thought until I'd heard someone from my local moot say they were going to drill for coalbed methane at Barton Moss, in Salford, which was about 15 miles from my home, and some of them were going to see what was happening. There was talk of a camp being set up by seasoned activists and locals, and they wanted to be involved.

I knew very little about fracking and so that evening embarked upon a crash course on the internet. The effects it would have on my water, home, health and the land around me shocked me to the core, and so I headed off to camp on a cold November morning armed with a big pan of vegetable curry and rice to feed the growing army of protestors who were setting up tents and caravans on the side of a country lane.

I was amazed that people were prepared to camp out in the cold, damp peaty lands of Barton Moss for the winter and I had little idea what to expect. The moss lands of Salford are an ancient place with peat that is 24ft-30ft deep and dates back to the Ice Age. It is also a harsh place to spend the winter, with ice cold winds and rain finding easy passage across these flat farmlands. The motorway provides a constant background noise that is interspersed with small aircraft taking off from an airport nearby.

A few weeks after regularly visiting camp with pans of food, herbal creams and elderberry rob, I plucked up enough courage for a slow walk of the trucks that were bringing the rig, water and chemicals to the drilling pad. Being a law-abiding citizen, I had few encounters with the police prior to this. I felt shocked at the large police presence on site, many of whom were pushing and shoving the protestors, making regular arrests and often causing injury. Walking the line with my Goddess-loving sisters was a powerful experience. Linking arms and calling her in for protection and courage, we faced the police and tactical aid unit (TAU) and sang to her. Other people joined us and hummed. Afterwards they told us that our singing calmed their anger and changed the atmosphere of the walk. Despite the anger, anxiety and aggression of the slow walk, I always felt an unseen presence with us, protecting and watching. It was only later I found out that the Moss was the home of my ancestors of blood and bone and they had lived on the Moss for centuries.

As winter deepened; the weather at the Moss got colder, damper and harsher. Most people were camping in extreme conditions and suffering from stress due to their interactions with the police, regular intimidation and arrest. Many were living outside for the first time and away from home. In challenging conditions such as these, one gets close to people, and it soon became apparent that camp residents and those locals walking the trucks regularly were getting sick. They were suffering from chest infections, colds, skin problems, and urine and kidney infections. Stress levels were often high and camp residents had a poor diet, living off high levels of sugary food brought in by appreciative locals.

My initial reaction led me to pack up most of my dispensary in boxes and I opened a herbal clinic in the Geodome; a large tent used for meetings, storage and the occasional night's sleep for protectors away from the windy, wet weather. The clinic became very busy and I realised quickly that to continue running a clinic like this I would soon be bankrupt. Having heard of the generosity of Lush cosmetics, I applied for a grant of £750 for a basic dispensary and bottles. Within an hour my application had been successful and the money was in my account to buy herbs. Herbal colleagues Danielle Kay, Zoe Blackwell and Zoe Naylor soon came on board together with a donation of herbs from local clinics and herbalists.

The Barton Moss Herbal Clinic was birthed in the Geodome on a wet Wednesday afternoon in January 2014 and we became affectionately known as the Wild Sistas. Our dispensary was stored and displayed on a coffin, which was later used in a direct action. The clinic was cold, damp and dark. We worked around piles of old clothes, settees and boxes and everything had a reddish hue from the plastic walls. Within minutes of us opening clinic, it was filled with sick people, curious children, dogs, hilarity and herbal tea from the woodstove. A reporter from the Los Angeles press and a local film crew captured that first day in photos and film.

We dispensed tinctures, teas, creams, cough syrups, health advice, general nurturing and lots of first aid. Protectors who had been injured from interaction with the police wanted treatment for badly bruised ribs and groins, sprained wrists, and grazes. Many people did not use conventional healthcare for various reasons and preferred to stay outside the system. It soon became apparent that we were their primary healthcare practitioners, and were often asked to treat a wide variety of conditions, some of which were quite serious. People had great faith in what we did, compliance was good and the results of the herbs spectacular. We learned that herbs work quickly and effectively with those who work close to the land, protect it and rely on the medicine that the plants provide. I've come to believe that when we go out of our comfort zones and are prepared to make some kind of sacrifice of ourselves for the earth, the earth responds and works with us.

We ran the clinic once to twice a week through the winter, often working outside in the cold and damp when the Geodome was full with storage. It was hard work but fun, running our clinic from tents, hay bales and later a wooden storage shed. Many a time we dispensed medicines outside in the elements balanced on a gas cylinder when there was nowhere else to go. Police presence was a regular occurrence and often they stood by and watched as we worked. Our dispensary was once even raided and our medicines ridiculed, but nothing was taken.

All our consultations and medicines were provided free of charge to those who came to see us. We accepted some donations from locals and gratefully used money that we raised from crowdfunding to replenish our stock. Once we made it clear that there was no charge for what we provided, people had no reservations about coming to us and we became a valuable part of camp life. Clinic hours were sometimes long, cold and challenging, were often asked for help outside clinic hours, on demonstrations, via social media and anytime we showed our faces. Our clinic day sometimes started by slow walking the trucks and worked around direct actions and camp life.

Our famous 'Warriors Drops' were conceived early on in response to some of the trauma, stress and anger on the front line. Little dropper bottles of valerian, rose and skullcap with a few drops of Rescue Remedy were dispensed to many on the camp, and made a regular appearance on the frontline and before direct action. Protectors said that these really made a difference in calming them and cooling the anger of the conflict with the police. One man told me that the Warrior Drops took him from screaming at the police to calmly engaging with them. Another said it grounded him and reminded him why he was doing the protest. Others said it helped with headaches and insomnia, leaving him feeling relaxed and gave him support during extreme stress and anger. Interestingly enough the TAU hated the smell.

We continued to run the clinic for the duration of the protest camp. The camp was present for six months and more than 200 arrests were made. There were continued reports of police brutality and many suffered emotionally and physically from a long, cold, damp winter of living outside. People told us that they couldn't have got through the winter without us and that we saved their lives through challenging times.

In April 2014 the last trucks were escorted up the lane and the tents were taken down. In summer as comfrey, hops, mugwort, greater celandine and rosebay willowherb grew in abundance, all remains of the camp were erased. The protest delayed the drilling for a few months and shares were down. Local communities woke up to the effects of unconventional energy and came together to defend the land. Barton Moss was a transformative and challenging experience for many and we knew that we played a valuable role in supporting this growing community by providing a medicine that was not only effective, but also connected them to the land and nature.

A meeting of the Wild Sistas concluded that the dispensary needed a proper home and funding was acquired from 38 Degrees to buy a caravan, tow bar and frontier stove for warmth, hot water and herbal tea. Our new clinic caravan resided at Crawberry Hill, in Hull, over the summer of 2014, where we ran regular clinics for burnt-out protestors.

That summer also saw the setting up of a new camp at Davyhulme, in Manchester, a place not far from Barton Moss. This piece of derelict and toxic wasteland next to the Trafford Centre became the new focus for protest, drawing together the tribe of local activists. It was hard place to be. Chimneys belched out yellow toxic smoke, the motorway flyover provided constant background noise and fumes and the smell from the sewage works stuck to your nostrils and stayed there. Many of the protestors became sick and developed rashes. It's not a pretty place, yet many people were prepared to risk their health and subject themselves to violence from an eviction team with a very bad reputation. My role as camp herbalist was to distribute Warrior Drops and to try to provide effective medicines to help poisoned protectors when it is all over.

A profusion of St John's wort grew in swathes all over the desecrated earth. Rich in blood-red healing constituents, it stained my fingers when I rubbed the petals. This taught me that the earth responds to such violation and destruction by providing a healing plant that brings light into dark places. This lovely bright yellow flower in its abundance, is a supreme nerve tonic, anti-viral and supports the liver as well as being a magically protective plant. Just what the camp needed!

As the sun went down and an uncertain night drew in, I called in the old ones for protection and ministered calming medicines to those ready to do a lock onto a makeshift tower in the middle of the camp. It was that moment I felt the presence of the Goddess and the beauty of this toxic wasteland. Wherever we are, no matter how poisoned the land, it is still sacred, it is all part of her body and many of the protectors knew this and were prepared to risk their own safety. The camp was not evicted that night and eventually protectors left the camp a week later because of sickness.

After Davyhulme the work of the Wild Sistas continued by supporting camps at Crawberry hill, Upton in Cheshire, Borras in Wales and Duddelsden in Shropshire. Clinics were often busy seeing protectors and local people who came to support the camps. One of the Wild Sistas, Zoe Naylor, lives on camp and is able to support people onsite most of the time as we can only travel to camp every few weeks because of the distance. The caravan is lovely to work from, but often cold and dark in winter and when the sun goes down, when we have to work by torch-light. It's good to do this sometimes, as it reminds us of the seasons and brings us closer to nature. We've had a few teenage apprentices, which delight us; it is good to teach them and involve them in making medicines for camps. There's pleasure in knowing that what we teach now will sow the seeds for the future.

Although we don't often tell people we're Green Witches, like the wise women of old who lived at the edge of the village, we keep the secrets of those who come to us, hear their troubles, challenges and help people sort out their problems. We make our medicines from the land, do the odd charm and put a bit of healing magic in their medicines. We've even been asked to do impromptu rituals, such as a first moon time, and give support to people waking up and connecting to the spirituality of the land and the Goddess.

Supporting the camps has been one of the most powerful, profound and awesome experiences I have had. I have learned a lot about frontline herbalism and being a primary healthcare herbalist to a massive tribe of earth warriors. My herbal colleagues have become my much-loved sisters, and the ever-expanding camps and local supporters respect our work, experiencing the power of herbal medicine first hand. Since my dedication to Elen more than 18 months ago, I have followed her quicksilver paths and gone to where she required me to be. As a consequence my life has changed unbelievably, bringing in purpose, friendship and a new relationship. I know that service to her is often very challenging, she takes us to our edges and beyond in order to get the best from us. I believe that Neo-Paganism is not a passive path, we follow the old ones and they ask us to engage with this troubled world and be active. They require sacrifice in exchange for the gifts we ask them to bestow upon us. In our consumerist society we are taught to continually take with no thought of return, and this can often be the same with our spirituality. To invoke them is powerful indeed and this demands we give back.

When I think back to that wet afternoon in Essex, I understand why she did not want me to wear the antlers. When you dedicate to an Earth Goddess and vow to protect her land, its serious stuff! Her path for me was not about dressing up and looking the part, but going beyond my comfort zone and into the anger, aggression and dereliction with muddy boots, a waterproof coat and a big bottle of Warrior Drops. She taught me that the darkest places teach us the most, all the land is sacred even if it's a toxic wasteland in Davyhulme, and that there is an amazing tribe of warriors out there who are prepared to sacrifice anything to protect her land.

Living Presence in a Field of Living Presence: Practicing Contemplative Druidry

By James Nichol

The Context

At Samhain 2011 I launched myself on a path of 'contemplative exploration' within Druidry. My own life and practice had taken a contemplative turn, in a specific sense of the word 'contemplative', where contemplative experience is described in terms of mindfulness, concentration, intuition, tranquillity, 'flow', or communion – perhaps union – with the Divine. For me, a key feature of any contemplative life practice is clarity of intention and deepening of attention: not primarily what you do, but the way that you do it.

I'm now in the fourth year of contemplative exploration. During that time I've deepened my solo practice. I now also have a local group to work with as well. In October 2014 I published *Contemplative Inquiry: People, Practice and Potential,*[1] which was largely drawn from interviews with practicing Druids who have an interest in the topic. Together with others from my local group, I have begun offering a limited number of open events to people interested in our approach to contemplative practice.

Contemplative Druidry is not a distinct and separate form of Druidry. Contemplative practice in some form has always been part of modern Druidry, and may well have been included in ancient Druidry as well – Old Irish *dercad* means 'looking' with connotations of deep understanding and fixing the mind upon something in meditation. Later, contemplative prayer was a major feature of Celtic Christianity, including the use of the contemplative Jesus prayer generally better known in the Orthodox tradition than in the Latin West. My point in naming a contemplative thread within Druidry is to draw attention to resources perhaps underused or underemphasised in the modern movement – possibilities and potentials that ask for a more specific focus; forms of practice and relationship deserving increased care and attention. My hope is that contemplative Druidry will develop organically and have many faces, with a rich diversity matching that of the wider movement. I would not wish it to be one 'thing' and see no chance of any such outcome.

I've decided to specialise in the contemplative aspect of Druidry both for myself and as a service. My foremost resource for this is practice – solo and in group settings. So most of what follows in this account is focused on practice and its results. I also study contemplative traditions and their implications for the aesthetic, therapeutic, ethical and political domains.

Solo Practice

My solo practice is a contemplative inquiry. As such, it has known roots in the European Pagan past. Towards the end of his life, French philosopher Michel Foucault analysed texts from the ancient Greek and Roman worlds[2] investigating the wider issues of human agency. He describes how the injunction to 'know thyself' emerged in cultures where philosophy, spirituality and medicine were not fully distinguished from each other since each in its way concerned self-care and the good life. In particular he is keen to show philosophy at work before the 'Cartesian moment' that separated 'a *philosophy* of knowledge from a *spirituality* of the transformation of the subject's very being by his work on himself'. 'Knowing thyself' always involves work on the self (*askesis*) and a relational movement (*eros*) between subject and truth; once truth is opened up, it confers highly prized states of consciousness accorded names such as enlightenment (*gnosis*), beatitude or tranquillity.

This is the contemplative gold standard of the classical Pagan world. I like the focus on the good life – being in a *eudemonic* state, holistically happy and in harmony with our inner guides. I like the uniting of spiritual practice with the effort of inquiry and the work of healing. I like the support for agency, personal responsibility, self-cultivation and independence of mind. It is of course also true that the approach is highly self-referential and a product of elite culture. There is no felt sense of inter-connectedness and inter-dependence. There is no necessary sense of embodiment.

So the Greeks and Romans, while providing some cultural foundation, are not a perfect model for me, here and now. I have sought a practice that celebrates embodiment and encourages an awareness of inter-connectedness. A good side of living in a globalising culture is the availability of diverse cultural resources and excellent means of communication. This has allowed me to find teachers very easily, when I have felt the need for them, as well as information and literature. So I have been able to craft a practice that draws on my OBOD training, Buddhist mindfulness meditation, and physical/energetic work from a Tantric tradition and then to take personal responsibility for knitting the practice together as a coherent whole. In my current phase of life, I am able to enjoy a two-hour morning practice, including journaling at the end, which generally begins between 5am and 6am, pretty much every morning when I'm at home.

It works. From a self-care perspective, it is fairly reliable as a green anti-depressant and contributes to a sense of health, rejuvenation and longevity promotion. I appreciate that these are trivial goals from the standpoint of some traditions, but so long as I remember that I can be struck down by death or disability at any time, this aspect of life practice (I don't separate out a 'spiritual' realm) seems like healthy common sense.

At another level, the meditation makes me very aware of my fragility, my insubstantiality, my complete embeddedness in a web of interdependence, and the narrow limits of my usual consciousness and perception. I'm gradually becoming at peace with this and learning to navigate with this understanding in mind.

At another level again, there are times when I almost melt with love and gratitude for the miracle of being alive at all. I am well aware the price of life is to feed on other life and to be at risk of the same fate – as a significant part of the interdependence. Yet I experience the prize – life – as an extraordinary gift, and am moved too by the world's seeming ability to be 'irrationally generous as well as unfairly hurtful'.[3]

I also notice that I am gradually losing attachment to my ideas and opinions, not the ideas and opinions themselves, but my investment in them. As one of the educated poor, these have been among my most prized possessions. Thoughts, ideas, systems have their place – but they don't matter as they once did. For instance: the more I practise, the more agnostic I become about heroic spiritualities. The older I grow, the more sceptical I become about the Jungian individuation epic (and the wisdom of later life), which once entranced me. These aren't hostile scepticisms, or a turning against the old ideas – I simply feel a withdrawal of energy and attention from them.

Overall, I loosely hold a view of panpsychism (preferring the word to its near neighbour animism). I experience myself as living presence in a field of living presence, and am nourished by the sense that 'every rock has Buddha nature'. If nothing else, this makes me more respectful and relational, more present to what is. It makes an 'ethics of empathy'[4] more natural. I think also that the buzz of the 'psych' word, its hinterland of association, reminds me of the possibilities of generally unseen, unapprehended as well as visible and obvious nature. Yet within this, I hold to a 'vulnerability of openness'[5] as the overall stance of my contemplative inquiry, parsimonious on matters of ideology and belief.

Our Group Practice

My local group in Gloucestershire, England, has developed a version of contemplative Druidry with two containers for group practice. One is the contemplative day, held twice a year. Days run from 10.30am to 4.30pm. The other is the two-hour session, held during every calendar month when we don't have a day.

Overall our practices are simple and spacious, limited to providing some structure and the opening up of possibilities. Ritual opening and closure of the space are important to us in dedicating the space and defining and enacting our intent, with a ritual design that tends to be light and minimalist. Specific practices include periods of sitting meditation; chanting *awen* and chants from the Ceile De *Fonn* repertoire[6] and other sources; and contemplative walking outside – especially on the full days where the walks can last for 90 minutes or more.

'*Awen* space', which began with a nod in the direction of Quaker meetings, has slowly evolved over the life of the group and become a defining practice. It is open-ended, though it tends to last for 35-40 minutes. We lead ourselves into and out of this space through *awen* chanting at the beginning and at the end. We open ourselves, becoming more receptive and sensitive, more present to whatever is in us, between us and in the space. Whatever follows will be whatever it is. We are not striving for special experiences or specific outcomes. That's the paradoxical magic of the space. Sometimes we sit in silence for all or most of the time – a silence that is aware of companionship and a group presence. Sometimes we chant, talk or sing into the space, surrounded by silent attention, which continues into the after echo of the contribution and moves again into a general silence. Sometimes we spark off each other almost to the point of conversation. But we keep out of conversation proper and above all make sure of not talking over each other.

I find this experience rich and others report the same. For me there are two aspects to this practice – the time itself, and an afterglow of both refreshment and connection. My sense is that we are offering each other an unusual quality of attention – unusual certainly in this culture of perpetual busyness – and that we can become recharged and replenished by that alone. But it also seems as if, at times, something else is present in the space as well. I can't define it and don't really know what to call it. In our group, because it is a Druid group, we call it *awen*.

Throughout our time in the group we share our experiences freely and without presuppositions about their value. This benefits us as individuals. It also acts as a means of co-creating group culture, learning as we go. Everything we do is both experiential and experimental, since we are not following pre-set forms or any established system.

Endnote

I am not a monastic or a hermit. These practices are not the whole of my life. Much of their value is the way in which they infuse the rest of the time, to a greater or lesser extent. For me this infusion isn't about particular meditative states – I also place quite a high value on down time and daydreaming, and only rarely do I follow myself consciously into sleep. What matters to me is to be in touch with that sense of being living presence in a field of living presence, of this being remarkable and to be celebrated, and having implications for how I do life. I have not set myself up as an evangelist for contemplative Druidry, but I hope that in this brief space I have managed to convey a sense of what it means to me.

References

1. Nichol, J. (2014) *Contemplative Druidry: People, Practice and Potential* Amazon/KDP (Foreword 'Deep peace of the quiet Earth: The Nature Mysticism of Druidry' by Philip Carr-Gomm).
2. Foucault, M. (2001) *The Hermeneutics of the Subject: Lectures*

at the College de France 1981-1982 New York, NY: Palgrave Macmillan (English series editor Arnold I. Davidson).

3. http://www.newstatesman.com/culture/2014/12/rowan-williams-why-we-need-fairy-tales-now-more-ever.
4. Batchelor, S. (1998) *Buddhism Without Beliefs: A Contemporary Guide to Awakening* London: Bloomsbury Publishing.
5. Reason, P. (1994) *Future Participation In Reason,* P. (ed.) *Participation in Human Inquiry* Chapter 3, 30-39 London: Sage.
6. http://www.ceilede.co.uk/company/the-fonn.

Living Ancestors – Honouring the Not Yet Dead

By Jo Ashbeth Coffey

There is much talk in many Pagan circles of ancestors, of reverence, of crediting their wisdom, being inspired by the different ages they lived through and all that study of their lives can tell us. There is a beauty in finding out details of residents of a Stone Age site or of a Medieval distant relative, and finding common ground.

There is even more, often overlooked, wonder in our ancestors who are still with us. We have as much to learn from our grandparents and great aunts, our elderly neighbours and friends from a different era as from those who lived aeons ago.

If we consider the ancient ancestors key to ourselves, then the chain leading back to them is surely essential to understanding ourselves and how we relate to them. Therefore our very own granny is a very special connection: she is from a past age, and yet she is still here, here to tell us what it was like; a living opportunity for us to show our respect and reverence for our ancestry in person.

I see Pagans easily raise a glass to ancestors and thank them, and I sometimes wonder how often they also make time to make a cuppa for their granddad and listen to his stories and thank him, and how often he is just a grumpy old man who talks too slowly for their impatience to let them really listen.

I come at Paganism from a Druidic angle; a Druidry with strong values around respecting and remembering ancestors, and most essentially of walking our talk. I am a member of OBOD and combine that with other elements I have learnt over the years; learnt from places such as counselling training and a degree-level life coaching course, and from who knows how many self-help books about making your life just right and being truly happy. The importance of those two aspects for me has shaped into 'Pragmatic Druidry', which effectively says: be conscious of our choices; aim for the best and highest ideals; but know that we all get there through little every day acts, small adjustments to habits, one tweak at a time, and as much as we can manage today is enough for now. (More on that process some other time).

In this article I consider how we can make small adjustments to our regular routines and changes in our everyday life. These changes are to reflect the reverence and respect for elders and ancestors that Druids speak of so highly in our rituals and definitions of our belief system's values.

Living Ancestors

Firstly, let's make it clear: the recipients, although I speak of nannas and grandpas, of great aunts and elderly cousins, these people do not have to be direct blood relatives. You certainly don't have to have inherited genetic material from them (though it does have a special magic of its own where you do share a bloodline and you can see physical resemblance through the ages). Nor do they have to be elderly. Your mother and father are your direct connect to your ancestral chain. Nor do you have to be related at all; we all have common ground of being people, humans, and if you've met a person you already have something else in common with them, whether it be where you live or some hobby or interest you share. An elderly neighbour who you learn to share with can easily fill the role of a social ancestor if not a genetic antecedent, as well as being a friend.

Actions Speak Much Louder Than Words

I would urge everyone to find their own ways of working that suit them, but would like to offer up a few as starting points or inspiration. Find new ones for yourself.

Write to People

Up until she died two days ago, I wrote to my mother's mother on a roughly weekly basis. She was an active woman for as long as she could be, but when she reached her 90s her ability to go out (to bridge club events, coach trips and the University of the Third Age) started to be restricted. I was aware of this and I decided that as I couldn't manage to visit her regularly (she lived hundreds of miles away) I would visit in spirit and do what I could to lift her day. I regularly chose a colourful, cheerful, usually floral (she loved bright flowers) greetings card or notelet, or coloured writing paper, part chosen through my taste, but primarily as something I thought she would enjoy and be cheered by.

To start with I had no idea what I was going to write except, 'Hello, I hope you're well,' and for occasional cards I wrote little more than that. But still they were sent. Soon though I was asking after her and telling her all about what we'd been up to lately; what storytellings my partner was doing; how my dance classes were going. To someone who is in the same house all day every day, and who doesn't have much company visiting, even just a short note is a lift to their day, a reminder they aren't forgotten. In this day and age of instant electronic communication there is something special and lasting about a physical notelet that doesn't disappear when powered off, and is more familiar to older generations. Often writing back isn't an option if there are hand or eye problems, though if that is the case when it happens it can become very special to you. Most importantly you are showing respect and doing something practical to make your living ancestor's life a bit better and building a connection between you.

Friendly Visits

If you live nearer you can choose to regularly call round for a cup of tea, or share a meal with your relative – I know I would have loved to have been able to do that with my family. If you have the opportunity – take it. It doesn't have to be a big palaver and the kind of scheduling that gives stress. Just dropping in, with a little forewarning, for a tea and a hello can build connections and reduce one of the greatest problems for older generations – loneliness. Then you get the wonderful extra part of listening to them and learning from them too. It is a chance to absorb their wisdom, and I urge you to listen, to let it wash over you and through the words find out who they are and what matters to them, be interested in how their life differs from yours. If you know yourself well you will soon find you are recognising where some of yourself came from. If you don't know yourself so well, the familiarity of their traits and behaviours might start to change that.

Speak and Listen

If writing and visiting don't appeal for whatever reason, then for many a weekly phone call is a great way to keep in touch. Let it be part of your routine, but do try to make sure you aren't phoning while doing other things, which means they don't get your attention. If you are calling someone to show them respect and friendship and help stop them feeling isolated, because they are part of your ancestry and you care, then don't do it half heartedly while it distracts you from the weekly shopping. Give them the proper attention they deserve, give them the focus you would a ritual.

Speak Out

We live in a time when a very large proportion of our elderly are dependent on social care and strangers for their personal needs. Homes are being closed, the media is rocked regularly by new revelations of elder abuse. We can all show due respect to all our living ancestors by campaigning, supporting campaigns, signing petitions and generally showing those making decisions that we are watching and we care what happens to elder-care.

Visit Homes

If you have very few accessible surviving relatives of your own and no obvious neighbours, but have the time and would like to connect, how about volunteering to visit at a local home? Around the country there must be thousands of childless older folks who don't have families of their own to visit who would like someone to keep them connected to the world outside their circle. It does us all good to connect with people outside our own age range and lifestyle. It does us good individually, and it does us good as a whole, as it creates a more compassionate, understanding society.

Live It

For some of us there is the opportunity and responsibility to actually live with older generations. If you have that chance then find joy in it, don't focus on the burden or inconveniences – make the most of the opportunity. It's not always easy living with those who have slower legs, hands or memories, but patience is the respectful response, and most of us are better off for learning to take things more slowly some of the time.

Pass It On Down

Teach your kids to value their grandparents. You may have had conflicts with your parents, but remember, unless they are very damaged people who still want to vent their pain on others, which is fairly rare, then they are likely to have a better relationship with their grandchildren. In being a significant part of their grandchildren's lives they enrich your children's lives massively as well as their own. Grandparents are the connection to a past, historic age for your children.

Count Everyone – Leave No-One Behind

Consider all the elders in your life: How many can you list in your life who you would call on as a wise elder? How many older relatives do you have? How involved in your life are they? How involved are you in theirs? Do you have relatives down the chain to encourage connection with?

Do Stuff

The media sometimes reminds us in the worst weather to check on older neighbours and do their shopping for them, but why wait until you're snowed in? Offering to pick up some shopping on your way back from work can be a real help to a less mobile older friend. Or do you drive? Can you help your older friend take their pet to the vet? Showing care and interest for things other people care about is a great way to build genuine friendships.

One Step Removed

On a less personal level you can still help and show your respect. How about volunteering for Age UK or other age-related charities? Help out in a charity shop or at a drop-in centre, or do fundraising. Drop-in centres welcome those with training to offer massages to tired old hunched shoulders, or offer organised activities. Many age-related charities are run at a local level, so you may have to ask around and search locally to find the one that works for you.

Listen

A key element of respect is, of course, to try to find out what that person would actually like from you, what will make them feel happier and more valued. Sometimes directly asking is a good idea, sometimes it's a matter of offering a few small kindness and seeing which seems most helpful.

I intentionally don't say 'see which is most appreciated'. If someone is in frequent pain from age-related conditions a grumpy manner can become normal. It's a way of venting the frustration the pain causes – it can be healthy to vent rather than bottle it up, think of it as therapy letting someone have a grumble at you, then gradually either help resolve it or lead on to happier subjects. Even just the frustrations of a shrinking life can turn grumbling into a habit. To those who aren't aware, it may not seem obvious that things are still appreciated. That said, of course you're not doing it for their gratitude anyway. Sometimes it takes feedback from a carer or other family member to let you know that it really does make a difference – listen to them too. Certainly don't line yourself up for abuse, but also remember not to take a sourpuss attitude as being about you, or something you need to fix, that's not respect.

Whatever you do – awareness and choice are key. Make Pragmatic Druidry choices of things you personally can realistically achieve. Do what you can, when you can, but choose to do it. Make your actions little steps on the way to your ideal goals. Be satisfied that you aren't perfect (none of us are) but know, having done something, that you have done as well as you can, and any mistakes will be learnt from. Most importantly, if your own values say you respect your elders, and value your ancestors, then show that to them in action, especially to the not yet dead ones. When it comes down to it, they're the ones who will really notice it the most, and for whom your effort and attention can really make a qualitative difference in their lives, as well as, most probably, in your own.

Passing on My Paganism: Being Pagan in a Multifaith Home

By John Halstead

I had called myself a 'Pagan' for years, but I don't think I really became Pagan until one August morning, standing in the waters of Lake Michigan with my Mormon wife, while we invoked the Pagan Goddess and baptised our two children. To this day, for me, being Pagan is inextricably intertwined with being a husband and a father in our multifaith home.

I was raised Mormon, went on a proselytising mission in Brazil for the Latter-day Saint Church (LDS), and went to college at Brigham Young University in Utah, where I met and married my wife in an LDS temple. When we moved to Indiana for me to attend law school, I left the Mormon Church. I then wandered for a while, spiritually, before coming home to Paganism. Meanwhile, my wife remained Mormon and took our children to the LDS Church.

I was a solitary Pagan, in more ways than one. I was reluctant to share my strange new religion with my wife and children for a long time. It was the impending baptism of my daughter in the Mormon Church, when she turned eight years old, that shifted me out of my spiritual solitude. I realised that, if I wanted our children to appreciate religious choices other than Mormonism, I had to present them with some.

My wife was very supportive when I suggested the idea of doing some kind of parallel Pagan ritual for our daughter. We discussed options with our daughter and settled on a 'Pagan baptism'. I had never heard of such a thing, and was aware that most Pagans tend to eschew anything that resembles Christianity too much. But my Paganism had always been highly eclectic, and the idea of reclaiming the traditionally Christian symbolism of immersion in water was appealing to me.

I think of ritual immersion in water as a potentially powerful, but symbolically neutral, ritual tool, that can be given new meaning in a Pagan context. The word 'baptism' simply means immersion or dipping in liquid. In our Pagan baptism, the water was to represent the womb of the Goddess, and immersion was to represent, not washing away sins, but a return to the source of all life — as all life began in the oceans. Of course, I thought, a Pagan baptism had to take place in a natural body of water, not in a baptismal font like Mormons use.

So we all went to the dunes at Lake Michigan early one morning in August and strode out into the still chilly water. We gave our son, who was 12, the option of being baptised too, so he didn't feel left out, and he readily agreed. We all wore T-shirts that said 'Jesus Loves the Little Pagans' depicting children dancing in a circle. My wife's Mormon parents attended, as did my agnostic father and atheist uncle, who were all supportive (if maybe a little bewildered). We began by singing Peter Mayer's 'Blue Boat Home': 'The wide universe is the ocean I travel, And the Earth is my blue boat home…' My wife and I stood the water with each of our children in turn, and said a prayer I had written, inspired by Goethe and Tielhard de Chardin:

> She is the womb and the tomb:
> An eternal ocean; changing, glowing, roaring, life in ferment.
> Like the swirling of life, she rises and falls:
> From her all things come, and to her all things must return.
> Son/Daughter of earth, plunge yourself into the sea of matter,
> Which is her body, for it cradled you long ago.

To which our children replied: 'She has been with me from the beginning, and she will be with me until the end.'

Then we laid each of our children back into the water and brought them out again. My wife and I felt inspired to join them, so we dunked ourselves as well. We spent the rest of the morning playing on the beach and flying kites. It was a perfect day. The next day, our daughter was also baptised in the LDS church, as my son had already been.

Ironically, that day on the beach, I felt like I had finally filled the role of a religious parent, which the Mormon Church had set before me years before. Since then, I've become more involved in the Pagan community, attending public Pagan rituals and Pagan festivals and conferences, at which I have been a presenter. I write for two well known online Pagan forums, Patheos and Witches & Pagans. And I am the managing editor of a community blog for Humanistic Pagans. But I never feel more authentically Pagan than when I am sharing my faith with my wife and children.

On Sundays, our kids go to either the LDS or Unitarian churches and they participate in youth programs at both. I have tried to educate our kids a little about the variety of world religions. They've been to Catholic, Orthodox, and Protestant churches, to a Reform Jewish temple, a Hindu Holi celebration, and a Native American ritual. I'm a firm believer that giving our kids a choice in religious matters means they have to be presented with real options, not just left to wander without direction. This means not only exposing them to a diversity of religions, but also sharing my own spirituality with them.

Since that day on the beach, I've created Pagan prayers for meals and bedtimes for our kids. I've also designed and led my family in rituals for all eight stations of the Wheel of the Year. I am particularly proud of our May Day ritual, as it brings together the Pagan and Christian faiths of our household. In the ritual, our children enact a drama in which Jesus and 'Magdala' try to get their parents, the Christian God and the Pagan Goddess, to stop their millennia-long argument and reconcile. Jesus and Magdala each exchange three gifts, which they then present to their same-sexed parent: earth, water, and air for the

Christian God, and a star, broken bread, and a wooden cross for the Pagan Goddess, each of whom find new meaning in these symbols, and the two come together.

Both of our kids, now in their teens, still enjoy our Pagan rituals, but neither of them actually identifies as Pagan right now, or Mormon for that matter. Our son is a staunch atheist and our daughter believes in reincarnation and karma and doesn't like labels. But more than a Pagan identity, I hope that our children will embrace certain values that I identify as Pagan, although they are not exclusive to Paganism. These include:

1. Humility and scepticism of claims to absolute, unconditional truth or other forms of religious exclusivism.
2. Respect for other religions and other people's religious experiences.
3. A feminist consciousness that appreciates how patriarchy has shaped the way we think and live.
4. Equality in all social relations, regardless of gender, race, or sexual orientation.
5. An ethics based on wholeness and healing rather than sin and purity.
6. A healthy attitude about their bodies and sexuality.
7. An experience of the divinity that can be found within themselves.
8. An experience of the divinity that can be found in nature.
9. An appreciation for myth and ritual as vehicles for connecting with the divine.

I look at my children today, and I know that, in this regard, and so many others, we have succeeded as both Pagan and Mormon parents.

Walking the Modern Minoan Path

By Laura Perry

'Do people really do that sort of thing?' That's the question I'm often asked when I tell folks, even fellow Pagans, that I follow a Minoan spiritual path. It's certainly a relevant question. This is the 21st century, after all; the last vestiges of Minoan civilization disappeared more than 3,000 years ago. In fact, the very existence of Minoan culture and spirituality had pretty much dropped off the map until Sir Arthur Evans began to dig up the ancient site of Knossos on the island of Crete at the turn of the 20th century. It's not like Celtic culture, which has stayed alive through a succession of folkloric revivals, or Hellenic Greek mythology, which has been a mainstay of classical education for centuries. So I'm often left explaining not only why I focus on Minoan deities in my spiritual practice, but what constitutes Minoan mythology and culture in the first place.

Amazingly, this spirituality that was lost to the world for so long and that flourished so many millennia ago is remarkably relevant today. That's what drew me to it in the first place. Unlike some later civilizations, such as classical Greece and Rome, on ancient Crete women were equal to men. They ran businesses, owned property and held high office. The Minoans had no military (except possibly a merchant marine) and hence no war gods, but they had a plethora of nature deities who helped them connect with the earth around them as well as shamanic deities who helped them find healing and insight and maintain a connection with their ancestors. To me, these are valid and valuable activities today. After all, how can we protect nature if we don't feel a connection to it? And how can we heal our own shadow sides unless we have access to them?

The Minoan pantheon is headed by goddesses who stand

alone – the Great Mother Rhea, Grandmother Ocean Posidaeja and Great Cosmic Mother-of-All Urania. But Crete was not a matriarchy in the sense of women 'ruling over' men and degrading them. It was an egalitarian society, a concept that shows in the pantheon, with all its equal goddess-god pairs such as Ariadne and Dionysos or Britomartis and the Moon-Stag. Of course, the issues of independence and interdependence have relevance for those of us today who are working for social justice and equality across a broad spectrum of issues.

The second question I usually get, after the person I'm talking to understands that, yes, people do actually practice Minoan Paganism, is, 'So what do you do?' If I'm really honest, I don't have one easy answer to give them. Much of what I do is an outgrowth of my lifelong exploration of Minoan spirituality and I often find myself being pulled in different directions. I have to balance ancient versus modern values as well as considering what kinds of religious activities contemporary Pagans are comfortable with. After all, what's the point of any kind of spirituality if it's not relevant to modern-day practitioners?

When I first discovered Minoan spirituality back in high school, thanks to an art history teacher who shared the beautiful Knossos frescoes with the class, I felt very alone. It wasn't until several years later, when I encountered the Pagan community, that I realised other people thought along the same lines and had similar worldviews. But I was still the only person who focused on the Minoan pantheon. Sometimes I wondered if what I was doing was okay. After all, I didn't have anyone else to tell me this was an approved path. I guess you could say the gods spoke to me, but the people didn't, and that can be a disconcerting feeling.

Eventually I discovered the concept of reconstructionism within Pagan spirituality. I was really impressed with what the Norse, Celtic and Hellenic reconstructionists were doing. That seemed to be the way to go with the Minoan path until I realised that most Pagan reconstruction is based on texts from the pertinent cultures. Guess what we don't have from ancient Crete? We can't even read Linear A, the script that records the Minoans' native language, and even if we could, there are very few inscriptions available, certainly not enough to provide deep insights into the Minoan mythology. And the few Linear B texts we have, written in Mycenaean Greek, are essentially just inventory logs. No great spiritual literature there. Sure, there are tales of the Minoan deities recorded in later Greek writings, but they were subjected to some serious revisionism by the Hellenic Greeks, who wanted to put women (and goddesses) in their place and make their own culture seem ancient and impressive. They're not exactly trustworthy sources.

So what's left as a resource for Minoan spirituality? That dreaded method – unverified personal gnosis (UPG). In other words, listening to whatever the gods have to tell you. We don't really have any religious texts to test UPG against for ancient Crete, but I've been gratified to see the amazing work the Norse reconstructionists have done with shared personal gnosis. This is a technique that involves a number of people independently experiencing an aspect of the spirituality then corroborating their experiences with each other. In some cases, this has been done with hundreds of people in the Norse traditions and leads to pretty secure additions to the spiritual practice. So a big part of what I do involves sharing personal experiences with the other members of the Minoan spirituality community in order to build up a tradition that works for us but maintains a certain amount of cohesion to what we know about the religion of ancient Crete.

In addition to the constantly evolving labour of shared gnosis, my personal practice has developed over the years to involve a collection of different aspects that I have to work to hold together. These aspects are in tension with each other, but are also integrated to some extent. I'm working with a spiritual practice that is truly ancient, that ended three millennia ago and that was pretty much forgotten for centuries, but I'm also working in the context of 21st century Paganism. Whatever I do has to be relevant to my worldview as a modern woman and that can be tricky.

Luckily, it turns out there are lots of people who are interested in Minoan spirituality who are walking this journey with me. Of course, they want to actually practice it, not just read about what might have been done 3,500 years ago. The liturgy, the rituals and the mythology have to have some basis in historical fact, even though the collection of historical facts we have is pretty slim, but it also has to feel right on an intuitive level to me and my fellow practitioners. That's a lot of directions to be pulled in at once. How do I deal with it?

I work very hard to listen to what the gods are telling me – there's UPG again. I have discovered that deities understand the passage of time, even if it does not directly affect them. They understand that we live in a world that is different in many ways from that of the ancient Minoans. We don't have temples and shrines we can go to when we want to worship, so we have to build our own sacred spaces in our homes, like the altar to Ariadne and the Melissae that graces my office. In our world, religion is considered a separate activity and not an integral facet of life, so we need specific lists of dates and occasions for rituals and other spiritual pursuits.

We don't know exactly what the format was for Minoan rituals, but we have to start somewhere. Wiccan ritual is familiar to most contemporary Pagans so I framed the ceremonies in my book *Ariadne's Thread* within a Wiccan-style setting (casting a circle, calling to the directions), but with tweaks to make the ceremonial style and details fit more closely with what we know about the Minoans' beliefs. When I do public ceremonies involving the Minoan pantheon, I do Wiccan-style rituals because I can be sure that format will be familiar and comfortable to the participants. But in private, I don't. Wicca and the Renaissance-era ceremonial magic that much of its form is drawn from didn't exist in ancient Crete. As far as we can tell, Minoan spirituality consisted largely of Mystery plays put on by the temples, shamanic workings by the professional priesthood, and visits by ordinary people to cave and mountaintop shrines. These are not exactly transferable to the modern world. So my personal practice is largely shamanic and when I have private students I instruct them in those methods. That's a bit of a tension right there, almost like there's a public version of Minoan spirituality along with a private version. But each is valid in its own way.

One day I'd love to put on a big Minoan-style Mystery play production for the greater Pagan community. I think people would feel a connection with the mythos simply by watching the stories being acted out right there in front of them. But until I can manage that, I have to take what I know about the Minoans and apply it to the life of a modern Pagan – me. I'm grateful for those who are willing to accompany me on the journey of discovery. And even when I feel like I'm stumbling, I'm pretty sure the gods are still smiling on us, simply because we care about them.

Magic and Science

By Brendan Howlin

At a first glance these two seem contradictory; how can our modern scientific method apply to something as esoteric as magic? However, if we delve a bit deeper we can find some interesting parallels.

The scientific method requires three things, i.e. a model, a means to test the model and a means to evaluate the results. The first of these might surprise non-scientists, as science is always presented as hard facts, but nothing could really be further from the truth. A model in this sense is a theory that fits most of the observable facts because we cannot really understand everything about what we are studying. In every scientific endeavour we use the current model for whatever we are studying until enough evidence accumulates against the model, so that we then need a new model. The example of this in action that most people are aware of is the rise of quantum physics, where the old model of classical mechanics, which people believed in for generations, was replaced with the new science of quantum mechanics. In essence the world appears to be classical to our interpretation, but it is really governed by quantum mechanics and the new model incorporates all the essential features of the old model. However, this is not to say that the new model is perfectly correct, there are still features in the new model that cause problems. We have no idea what new model will replace this at the moment, so have to wait for the evidence to accumulate.

Well, you might ask, what has this to do with magic? In magic, people believe in models, these models are called Wicca, Druidry, the Angelic Realms, etc. We interpret the world through our model just as people did with classical mechanics. It instantly leads to the important conclusion that it is perfectly valid to have a range of models that equally well fit our experience of the world. The proof of the pudding, as it were, comes in the second stage. Is your model testable? If you are ill and you pray to the Angels for healing and you then get better, you could be said to have tested your model. This is of course assuming that you would not have got better without the Angels' help. This is called a control in science and is something we obsess about. If you do something, can you compare it to the situation where you didn't do it?

Controls are the most difficult things to do in real life as you often can't do the control. In the above case there is only you and you don't know what would have happened in the alternative situation. Here, we have to bring in the problem of belief. It is a problem to scientists and the most well-known example is in the clinical trials of new drugs. In these trials most people are given the drug, but some are given sugar pills called placebos without being told which one they have been given. In some cases those taking the placebo have just as good responses as those taking the drug. This is the power of belief and is just the same these days as it was in the old days of the shaman healer, who if he/she told you to get well you would. There are also well documented cases of the reverse, particularly among the Aborigine peoples of Australia, where if the shaman told you that you were going to die, you did, even if there was nothing wrong with you in the first place.

In my tradition of Druidry we try not to do anything that will impact on the world in a negative way. To take this further, I am going to use this simple definition, which may upset some readers, but please bear with me. White magic is causing a change to yourself by the application of the will and black magic is affecting something or someone else by the application of the will. White magic is perfectly congruent with science and is often called psychology and/or psychotherapy; black magic can also be covered by science as in the following example.

If I am a 14-year-old girl and I want a certain boy to fall in love with me I could try a love spell. Having performed my spell, I know it has worked, so the boy is now in love with me. Flushed with my success I might actually start hanging around the boy and even talk to him. He will think, 'Who is this beautiful creature? She is obviously interested in me.' He may even fall in love with her as a result. Here, what appears to be black magic by my definition is actually white, because you have changed your own attitude and the magic has worked! To come back to the control, there is none in this case as you can't try it again without doing the spell.

Sometimes, the power of belief flies in the face of science, the classic example being the 100 Monkeys as popularised in Lyall Watson's 1979 book *Lifetide*. Here the theory is that if something is believed or practiced by 100 monkeys, all the rest of the monkeys automatically know about it or can do it. This was an icon of the Campaign for Nuclear Disarmament and is still widely promulgated these days. The attractive idea is, if a critical number of humans do or believe something then suddenly all the humans will do or believe it. It is a very attractive idea because it leads to the belief that a small number of people can change the world. However, the scientific observations that it is claimed to be based on never actually happened and Watson himself admitted that he had made it up for his book. Despite this, many people still believe passionately in this concept.

One of the main tenets of Druidry and also of many other traditions is the concept of the light body, which we switch on when we meditate. From a scientific point of view, one would say that this is obviously just in your own head as it is plainly obvious that human bodies do not emit light. If this was the case then we would glow in the dark. However, a few years ago a group of Japanese scientists decided to test this by putting people in dark rooms with ultrasensitive cameras trained on them. The results were remarkable as the subjects were shown to emit light, mostly from the head and face and this emission of light varied with the time of day. So here something that has always been believed as an article of faith was shown to have a scientific basis.

Scientific verification can also have its limits as in groups that do extensive rituals for world peace, for example. It is plainly obvious that meditating on world peace and giving your energy to it has not caused world peace to happen. This is purely obvious from observation, but many people suspend their disbelief and carry on regardless. If you change your own behaviour and show peace to everyone you meet, then you are working for world peace and may change the attitudes of those around you to be more peaceful and this effect will spread. Again this operates by my definition of white magic and is a scientific application of magic.

This brings me nicely to magical practices that cannot be verified scientifically. For instance if you have a dream where someone who is dead contacts you and wants you to help their soul to pass on, you can do a ritual to help them, but how do you know that the whole thing didn't just take place entirely in your own head? The ability of human beings to make things up is well documented and apparently limitless, hence the wide body of written fiction in the world.

So in summary, there are many instances where science and magic meet and many where they don't. The two concepts are not as alien to one another as one would first think and, as in my light body example, there are cases where science is discovering things that have long been accepted by magical practitioners. Arthur C. Clarke, the famous science fiction writer, said in his third law of prediction that, 'Any sufficiently advanced technology is indistinguishable from magic.' Perhaps we are getting there slowly.

Modern Pagan Life

By Rachel Patterson

When I looked at the subject for this essay, 'Modern Pagan life, being, believing and belonging in the 21st century', my initial thoughts were, 'Wow, this is a bit grown up for me', but actually it is just all about what I do on a daily basis.

I am a working mother and wife and also have a real job as a personal assistant (the one that pays the bills), but I am also a witch, an elder, an author and a high priestess, so how does it all fit in together? Well it's pretty busy all the time and occasionally downright hectic...but I wouldn't have it any other way. Whatever I am doing, whether I am hovering, dusting, cooking the dinner or typing a letter, I am a witch; it is what I am, who I am and how I live my life. Because while I am dusting I will probably also be chanting and smudging to dispel negative energy and bring in good positive vibes. Hey, I can multi-task...

In the days of the wise woman (or man, let's be politically correct here) life would have been a lot simpler, but a heck of a lot harder. They would have arisen when the sun did and gone to bed when the sun set, foraged in the fields and hedgerows for herbs and plants and lived in a cottage that required a wood fire to provide heat and to cook on. They would have spent time making salves and tinctures, dealt with local villagers coming for cures – and probably curses as well – and payment would have been bartering and exchanging of lotions and potions for food and clothing. In some ways it sounds peaceful and idyllic, but the winters would have been harsh, disease was rife and seriously there would not have been any sign of an en-suite bathroom...

So how does that differ to my life today? Well, I still work with herbs and plants that I grow in my garden. I definitely don't get up at sunrise, although not much later as I have the school run to do. I work magic, I perform rituals, I work healing, I meditate and I connect with spirit and the divine. I just do it sitting in my living room more often than sitting shamanically around an open fire in the middle of a field. I don't grow all my own food, my garden is way too small, but I do try to purchase from farmers directly. But then we also have the convenience of shops…if I run out of butter I can take a two-minute walk to the corner shop, I don't have to milk a cow and spend ages churning it to create my own.

We have all the mod cons – electricity, gas, showers, heating, cookers and the internet. We live in total luxury really and can connect with other Pagans or anyone else at the touch of a button.

Nature has not changed, putting aside pollution, erosion and man's tendency to trash it, but overall it has not. You can still stand on top of a mountain and feel the wind in your hair, you can still sit quietly in the middle of a forest and relish the silence and you can still stand on the beach and get lost in the hypnotic crashing of the waves…you just need to find a spot away from the pier and the ice-cream sellers…

When I started on this pathway many years ago it felt as if I had come home, I didn't know anyone else in the Pagan world so I started learning from books, witchcraft on the internet was in its infancy so I picked up bits and pieces from there too. Then I joined an online group and a whole world of like-minded people opened up to me. I also discovered via the internet that not only were lots of these people local to me, but there were also Pagan groups in my area too.

I learnt a lot from books and online courses, but I also learnt a whole heap load more by actually getting out there and being with people who were on a similar pathway to me, without the internet I would have struggled to find those connections.

My pathway has twisted and turned and been filled with life lessons, inspiration and total light-bulb moments. I have found I can share with others all of my experiences and lessons learnt, which is amazing.

I like a structure of learning; I am too undisciplined and easily distracted and it was via the internet that I connected with those that would teach me all I needed to know and more…and then to be guided off line and into the outside world to meet those people face to face to learn even more.

All of my training and experiences led me to set up, with others, our own online school of witchcraft and an offline coven that meets for open rituals. We have also run workshops locally and now run goddess and herb courses online too. Running the rituals locally in a beautiful countryside setting has allowed us to meet a lot of our students from online, to put faces to names has been fantastic and we have made so many wonderful friends.

Running the online school and online courses has allowed us to share what we have learned, to pass on the knowledge as a wise woman would have once done face to face with an apprentice, but the internet has allowed us to reach across the world and share with students from all sorts of different countries.

Inadvertently perhaps we have created our own Pagan community, filled with wonderful people who all support and encourage each other, and for that I feel truly blessed.

As for believing, well I guess our ancestors would have believed in gods of the sun, the moon and the earth because their whole livelihood, their whole existence relied on the sun coming up and the weather being kind for the crops. If the harvest was poor, chances are they would not survive the winter because they would have no food. We don't have to deal with those sorts of circumstances in the modern world; well in my country we don't. Unfortunately starvation still exists in other parts of the globe.

Does the whole god of the sun, sky and moon still translate and work in modern times? Well, I think it is all down to each person. I have met a lot of Pagans and each one will view deity and the divine in a different way. I love that it works for each individual in whatever way they see fit. We now have an understanding of science and how and why the sun rises and sets when it does; we don't have the fear that it won't rise the next day, but that doesn't and shouldn't stop us from honouring it and being thankful that it does.

It all boils down to personal faith. I have faith in the goddess that she will guide me in all that I do and she does in fact spend a lot of her time kicking my butt because I don't always listen, but I have faith that she is always right.

Does Paganism belong in the 21st century? Other than answering with a resounding yes, of course it does, why shouldn't it? We are a complete pick and mix of people across the world with a whole host of different religions, faiths and practices, why wouldn't one of the oldest religions still be current today? I think part of the attraction and reason that Paganism is still here and still works is because of its flexibility. There is no book of hard-and-fast rules, there are no main dictators enforcing how you practice or follow it. Paganism works for each individual as they want it to and there are so many different pathways within it, if one doesn't quite fit you can branch out into another or even as I do…take bits from all different pathways and blend them together to make your own personal brand.

We probably all feel the need on occasion to escape, to disappear from the madding crowds and the hustle and bustle of modern life and thankfully that is still possible, there are still places to go away from cities, traffic and people. But…and here is the thing, we do have the best of both worlds because we can also sit in our nice warm centrally heated houses and have hot running water for showers and baths, cook conveniently in our houses or even still outside if we want to. We can have that happy balance of retreating to our own solitude to just be or meditate or work our own spells and rituals or we can press a button or pick up a phone and meet up with others for rituals, moots, learning, sharing and general mischief and merriment. Basically we do have it all.

Ancient Roots, Modern Faith

By Morgan Daimler

In many ways being Pagan in the 21st century feels like walking in two worlds, one foot always in the world of cell phones, computers, and hard evidence while the other foot is firmly planted in a world of enchantment, myth, and intuition. Because of this there is an inherent feeling of liminality to my faith, which is both a blessing and a challenge. On the one hand having a balance between such diametrically opposed realities is a wonderful thing, which allows me to feel grounded and mystical at the same time; on the other hand finding that balance is sometimes a huge challenge, with each side pulling for my attention. I find that being a modern Pagan is often as much about facing internal and external challenges to my spirituality as it is about living that spirituality.

My own path is, perhaps, more difficult to live in this modern world because I'm a reconstructionist, which means that my religious practice and witchcraft are more strongly bound to the distant past than other people's might be. Reconstructionism is a methodology that can be applied to anything and is based on using archaeology, anthropology, mythology, and folklore to reconstruct older beliefs and practices. Relying heavily on historic precedent while remaining relevant and engaged in the world of today is a constant struggle, but one that I enjoy. I love the thrill of learning some new titbit of information about ancient belief or new fact about historic practice and then finding the best way to incorporate that information into my own life, whether that is simply tucking it away as knowledge to remember or putting it into active practice in my own life.

Being a reconstructionist to me means being on a perpetual quest to find every little piece I need to build the structure of my religion, like a bird weaving her nest one twig at a time. The experiential, living, breathing side of my faith then has room to live in this creation, using the structure as a solid base. This is important to me because my spirituality is something I live all day, every day; it is a part of who I am, and I cannot separate the daily practices from the daily experiences of my faith. I pray traditional prayers and make offerings and I feel the numinous. I reach out to the Gods and spirits as I understand them from academic study and I feel them reaching back, immanent and present, building that understanding into something deeper and stronger.

Another challenge that I struggle with is raising my children with my faith. It's important to me that my three children grow up with a strong sense of tradition, whether or not they ultimately choose to follow these traditions as adults. I myself was raised a secular agnostic and while my family lacked any religious traditions in my childhood, we did have many non-religious holiday practices, which I still value very much. I want my children to be able to look back on these years and remember our holidays and other spiritual practices fondly. My oldest daughter is very religiously inclined and has always enjoyed actively participating in what we do, since she was a toddler. I can't deny that this makes me happy, but it also creates problems for her, especially in school with her peers where she is often teased and accused of lying when she talks about her beliefs. This has necessitated a few visits to the school on my part and sadly has curbed her naturally outgoing personality. I have found it difficult to teach my children to be proud of their faith, but also to understand that other people will be prejudiced against them for it. Nonetheless my children are proud of who we are and what we believe, even when that brings them into conflict with the mainstream. And practicing my religion, especially holiday celebrations, with my family, has become an important part of my own religious practice.

My Gods are old and their stories resonate through time, speaking of things that will always be relevant to people: love and life, battle and death, healing and security. The words of their stories are archaic, but the message is timeless, and something that I think anyone can connect to when they hear it. When I first heard the stories of the Irish Gods, the Tuatha Dé Danann, they immediately resonated with me in a way that nothing else had. They fired my imagination and woke something in my soul; I felt as if those stories were reaching out to me across the ages and I had to reach back to them. And that is how I found the Gods. Ever since then I have continued to find the Gods in the old stories as well as in the world around me. I read about Flidais in the *Táin Bó Flidais*, but I also see her in meditations, and when I almost died after my youngest child was born she was the one who appeared to me and helped me get through the situation. I read about Nuada in the *Cath Maige Tuired*, but I also find him on the shore of my local river and hear his voice in my dreams. I read about the Morrigan, as Macha, Badb, and Morrigu, in the *Lebor Gabala Erenn*, but I also hear her voice in the call of crows and see her in the faces of her priestesses. The Gods, like my religion, are rooted in the past, but active and present in the world today as well. The Gods are so much a part of my life I can't actually wrap my head around the idea of anyone not being aware of their presence.

The one part of my spirituality that may be even more intrinsic than the Gods is the Good Neighbours, who most people call fairies. For me all things have a spirit, but there are also those Otherworldly spirits who choose to interact with our world, and these spirits are the bedrock of both my spiritual belief and my witchcraft. Although I should say that there is a blurry line at best between the Irish Gods and the Fair Folk, meaning that the divide between my Gods and the fairies is neither clear-cut nor easily defined. It's funny actually, or perhaps ironic, that as a modern Pagan there is more difficulty in honouring the Other Crowd now than in honouring the Gods. The Gods have in many ways stayed fundamentally the same and even those who have been altered by modern perceptions have not lost the connection to their origins, but the fairies have been so thoroughly sanitised and remade in most modern Pagan views as to have been re-invented entirely, so that the beings I honour are utterly unknown to other people using the same terms for them. This creates a huge disconnect and an interesting problem for me in relating both to non-Pagans, who often don't believe in the Good Neighbours at all, and other Pagans, who may believe in them, but have such an antithetical view to my own that we may as well be talking about entirely different things. In response to this I try to teach people when and where I can about the older views and beliefs and the traditional ways of honouring the fairies, not because I want everyone to agree with me, but because I don't want the old beliefs to die out or be subsumed. There is a lot of power and beauty in the old ways, in nurturing a friendship with the People of Peace built in respect and appreciation both for what they can bless us with and what they can do if angered. I do not want to see that lost.

My life as a modern Pagan is a complex tapestry of influences, some from the shadows of the distant past, some created with every breath I take, but I wouldn't have it any other way. It is a life full of challenges from the inside as I try to balance these diverse influences and from the outside as I struggle against the expectations and peer pressure of society and other Pagans. But, ultimately, it is my life, has been my life since I was very young, and it is a life I love. I may, long ago, have chosen the harder road to walk – or perhaps it chose me, if there was ever any choice involved – and yet I would not change a single thing about it. Being a modern Pagan isn't about fitting in to anyone's mould or blending in to a crowd, rather it's about finding your own voice and the courage to sing.

Passionate Paganism

By Robin Herne

The Victorians were in the habit of using the term 'pagan' as a euphemism for wanton and licentious behaviour. In 33 years of being Pagan I have to say that, if any of my fellow Pagans engage in wanton rituals, they have never bothered inviting me! A lifetime of bitterness to one side, modern Paganism tends to attract people for whom sexuality and/or gender are issues for consideration – such as homosexual, bisexual and transgender people, towards whom mainstream religions often have a history of hostility. This may be in part because we have a wide array of deities and other religious figures that are known to desire their own sex, to pair off with men and women alike, to change their genders, and so forth.

The Irish LGBT rights campaigner and drag performer Panti Bliss[1] has very eloquently and passionately summarised the experience of many people in the comparatively liberated western world of the 21st century (how much worse must it be for people in parts of the world where being gay or transgender often leads to prison, torture, or execution?) As Panti has said, straight couples seldom have to give a second thought to holding their partner's hand in public, or sharing a peck on the cheek – and, of course, a fair few don't give a second thought to all but sucking each other's fillings out regardless of where they are.

I decided to act on my sexual attraction to other men when in my early twenties, and have been conscious ever since of even the most minimal displays of affection to partners when in public. Even when at a party or other gathering where there were people present whose views on such matters were unknown to me, the wariness remains. I have never been 'gay bashed' or spat at, or subjected to any other kind of physical intimidation as a result of my sexuality. Yet I've heard the snide comments about queers and benders from so many people over the decades, and seen the news reports about people being assaulted, murdered, and driven to suicide so often that – like many, perhaps most, LGBT people – I have the internalised monitor that watches for threats. It polices what I do and what I say, just in case some random stranger (or even someone I know) feels it their social right to barrack or batter me. I do not wish to give the impression that I live in some state of abject terror, because it is nowhere on that level. One simply gets used to viewing other people as potentially hostile, and most of the time it doesn't really enter consciousness.

Most of the few occasions where I have been relaxed enough to give the internal monitor unpaid leave have been at Pagan gatherings. My initial involvement with Paganism started even before I had any conscious awareness of my own sexual preferences, so I cannot say that the atmosphere of tolerance was a key draw. However, it may well be one of the reasons why I stayed. To know that you are safe within a community is a rare thing for some of us, and something liable to be appreciated by anyone who lives with the threat of reprisal just because of who they are.

I am not suggesting that all Pagans are doyens of tolerance and openness. There are people who convert to Paganism yet retain their old bigotries, and I have met one or two of them. Thankfully they are in a minority. Rather than aggression towards LGBT people, it's more common to see lack of awareness. Within some Pagan traditions (and certainly in the sort of generic paganism popularised by countless books) there is an emphasis on gender polarity – the idea of there being a God and a Goddess of whom all other deities are but aspects. A large number of Pagans celebrate the Wheel of the Year, and for many of them this is narrated by the stories of this male-female couple.

There is nothing intrinsically wrong with this heterosexual story, but for those of us who relate more readily to our own sex, or who have no real interest in sex at all, or who are no longer the gender we were designated at birth, it can be a difficult story to fit with. The Pagans of the ancient world did not, so far as can be readily determined, follow this duolatry. They were polytheists with a vast number of stories about all manner of deities and pairings – deities coupling with their own sex, with both sexes, deities who were entirely self-contained and devoid of consorts, deities who changed sex, ones who were hermaphrodite etc. None of this is to deny the importance of heterosexual pairing to the reproduction of life for humans and most other species, but acknowledges that there is a great diversity out there and no single story tells it for everyone.

The Wheel and the God-Goddess story cycle that fits it is a modern adaptation created by selecting some elements (and ignoring others) of the myths and practices of a variety of ancient cultures. It suits many, but for those it does not so readily fit, the original cycles and stories are far more encompassing of human diversity.

Sometimes it can be difficult for people from minority sexualities and gender identities to readily blend into some forms of Pagan ritual, particularly ones that focus heavily on polarity. Of course, nobody is obliged to attend group rituals and one can be a perfectly happy Pagan in a solitary capacity – though that should be through conscious choice rather than a lack of other options. Rituals are rarely organised with the explicit intention of alienating individuals attending, so it is normally just lack of realisation that the symbolism used can often leave some people feeling cold. I have sometimes heard exponents of the 'mainstream' approach getting defensive when this is pointed out, and responding with the argument that everyone has a male and female side to their nature and should relate to the mythology in these terms.

Putting aside the somewhat dubious act of telling people how they ought to interpret a symbol in order to conform, such approaches are often accompanied by assumptions that need challenging. People who haven't met many gay or lesbian couples often assume that one partner is butch/masculine and the other is feminine, and that this plays out not just in terms of dress and mannerisms but also sexual acts. Obviously there are such couples around, but not all gays/lesbians fit into stereotypical echoes of heterosexual patterns. Even the ones who do may not engage in the sexual acts that other people assume. Gender and sexuality are complex and fluid aspects of human nature, and people seldom fit into neat little boxes.

Not all modern Pagan traditions focus on polarity. One of the appeals of druidry, for me, is that polarity really doesn't enter into it. My personal experience of druidry is that gender plays very little role in general. Within the past few years gender has become a prominent issue in some American Pagan circles, with female-only rituals bringing to the fore conflicting interpretations of who is a 'true' woman and permissible to attend. Gender-blindness is not automatically a good thing, and maybe some of us need to reflect more deeply on such issues as what gender actually is. Many ancient cultures held ideas around gender that went beyond biology, even where they lacked the medical skills to transform bodily appearance.

Rituals devoted to Zeus and Hera or Odin and Frig do not exclusively attract heterosexuals to their worship, yet it is not uncommon for a ritual honouring Antinous or Hermaphrodite (to name but two non-heterosexual deities) to only be attended by people from sexual or gender minorities. Pagans are still members of the wider culture and heirs to the same biases that influence everyone else, which includes the tendency to segregate. The assumption that 'gay gods' are only for gay people is hopefully a short-lived parochial view that will soon be replaced by the wider realisation that the transformative presence of a deity is not restricted to a certain category of person. Communing with a deity that embodies some aspect of our own nature can be a key moment in the process, to paraphrase George Bernard Shaw, not of finding ourselves but of creating ourselves. Though equally we should not restrict ourselves to that which is similar, or it might degenerate in autolatrism. Embracing that which is different transforms and evolves through challenge rather than reinforcement.

As Pagan religions continue to develop and adapt in the 21st century we will hopefully become more inclusive and embracing of the complexities of both human and divine nature.

Reference

1. Search YouTube for her broadcasts, they're worth listening to!

The Path of the Hearth Fire

By Sheena Cundy

Being Pagan, for me, is about growing. It's about relating to Nature as a teacher and guide, taking cues from her and tuning in. It's about connecting. I believe we all inherit the seeds of ancient wisdom and only by nurturing these seeds, by honouring all that she is – her cycles, the ebb and flow of her magical tides – do we learn.

Having just experienced one of those steep learning curves, I can see it was a much needed wake-up call from the Great Mother herself.

A call to stop, get a grip. Simplify.

Just before the end of 2014, we had a wood-burning stove installed into our home. We were excited and huddled round to watch its grand, debut performance. 'Much better than the telly,' I said to my husband.

Apart from being a great addition on a practical level, it is symbolic of something far more magical in the home. It has redefined my path.

The path of the Hearth Fire is a basic one – centred around the family and the home – and calls to us through the grind of daily life, to our responsibilities and our relationships. If we haven't learnt to prioritise, to concentrate on what really matters; the Hearth Fire shows us how.

It's a path of service and sacrifice, where the burden of obligation can weigh heavy. It's a path where we may have to put on hold any active involvement in the spiritual mainstream of our lives, and focus on the home and family.

But I never thought it was for me.

When I was 15, my father left the family home for a woman who lived round the corner. I don't blame him; ours wasn't a particularly happy house to live in. How could it be with two parents at war most of the time? Off he went and not long after, off I went. The big, wide world beckoned.

I kicked my heels up and began to roam, pursuing my love of horses and a career of 30 years. A typically Sagittarian outlook meant I *was* the centaur on an exciting journey and I galloped around – quite madly at times – on the lookout for adventure. Nothing and no-one was going to tie me down. But something was missing...a sense of belonging, I suppose.

Eventually, I found the path of the Hearth Fire.

For 17 years now, home has been a wild and windswept part of the Essex coastline, surrounded by large dollops of land, sky and sea. As often as possible, I escape to the beach with my dog and sit in the old 7th century Celtic chapel. It's a magical place, full of the spirit, where I sing, pray, send out healing to the planet and the people and then, fully revitalised, I return home and weave my writing in and around the chores.

As a stay-at-home mum, I have managed to use more of my time as the children have grown less dependent. This space has allowed my magical work to unfold, through writing, in song, story, and teaching and as a sister of the craft. Never before have I been so productive, so inspired by the magic all around and within me.

At last, I am free to express my creativity!

That was, until my mother-in-law came to stay…forever.

Perhaps a rain check from Mother Nature don't you think? A timely reminder to step down off that magical high horse – before it disappeared over the cosmic horizon – and keep those feet on the ground.

Well, it would seem the Crone had other ideas. I have come to know this wise old spirit guide quite well over time, she has come through with the best guidance in moments of great need and I bow to her innate wisdom.

I just wasn't expecting a real live one turning up on the

doorstep.

Nothing could have prepared me.

I kicked angrily against the situation for a while, frustration and resentment erupting in volcanic outbursts at anything and anyone. I was going off like a firework, in all directions. It was ugly.

I didn't know I had so much disgusting, emotional bile in me, but wait a minute…this wasn't fair, someone had just taken my space, my time!

No time to write, no space to write in, just a demanding third child and the endless stream of mundane chores and duties. It staggered me how one more person in the house could make such a difference. It was enough to drive anyone to drink and drugs – both of which I leaned towards in wobbly moments. This was taking grounded to a whole new level I'd never experienced before, and it scared the hell out of me.

I had to find a way of coping that didn't involve solvent abuse, packing a suitcase or a murder weapon – there didn't seem to be a healthy option. At times I thought I was going quite mad. Caught in its stranglehold, how I despised the path of the Hearth Fire and how I hated Mother Nature for the bitch she could be.

I had to find another way, and already up to my neck in the mundane, it was hard to see the magical, although I knew if I asked, the help would come. And it did.

Things began to look different.

The demanding third child became the Divine Mother calling me to honour the mother and the passing of years. The needy and dependent old lady turned Wise Elder and called me to honour all wisdom gained through experience. And the angry and selfish old biddy was the Crone Goddess, encouraging me to face my fears and learn to trust.

Everything changed.

Muriel is 91, has rheumatoid arthritis and is constantly in some kind of pain. Tablets are not without their side-effects and she has always enjoyed hands on healing. So I set the healing temple up in the living room where she likes to sit and I give her healing. It helps. It's the least I can do for her on a practical level and yet the most beneficial, spiritually.

Our situation is much improved with this regular spiritual prescription of compassion and forgiveness. The human spirit is a magical thing.

Acceptance takes a while of course, but the side effect is that it filters into other areas too and everyone benefits. The lessons of the Hearth Fire can be a tough discipline and my husband's prophecy of, 'We'll laugh about it one day,' remains to be seen, although he's usually right and we usually do.

I planted seeds of peace at Imbolc, for the highest good of all. How lovely that Brigid in all Her Hearth Fire glory breathed the flames of healing and inspiration into them. With so much focus on one family member, in need of a lot of care, the impact on the whole family (and not just the deranged daughter-in-law) can't be avoided. What happens to a part, affects the whole and change is ever constant. But it would seem the magical tides are flowing in the right direction now as we make plans for Muriel to go into permanent care, just round the corner in our village.

It is the right thing to do for the family and I'm looking forward to spending more time with my husband and children, to getting back to being creative.

To some degree, the Hearth Fire path calls to us all at some level. Whether it's the cry of a needy family member or the pleading of the Hoover from a dusty corner…its presence is underlying and its power cannot be underestimated.

How we respond to it is the important thing and what we take from it can be the most empowering lesson. One learns to be as flexible as possible. I have formulated rituals, cast circles and performed spells in my head quite effectively while attending to the most monotonous of tasks. And, as every modern witch knows, improvisation is a necessary skill in this day and age.

After all, the most powerful, magical tool we have is our mind and the sharper we keep it, the more potent our magic will be.

Balance is everything, and the Hearth Fire demands nothing less.

Whether we stumble onto it or set foot upon this path with conscious intention, I have come to believe it is an initiation of the body and soul no less than any other. No book will teach what experience can do better.

So, however lofty our aspirations, however much we struggle against it, like I did, if we make a ritual out of every humble duty and honour the sacred space of the home then it truly becomes a temple…and the Hearth Fire path will lead us to the door.

Authentic Shamanism

By Yvonne Ryves

Shamanism and the title of shaman, if used in its original context, only really relates to the Tungus people of Siberia not to any other culture, but those of us who work with shamanism now use these terms as a way to describe what we do. Shamanism is therefore no longer thought of as being restricted to any single culture. Historically, shamanic practice grew within cultures independent of each other and even if the names of those who worked shamanically were different – for example; witch, medicine man or woman, sin eater, or wise one – they could all be considered to be forms of what we now would term as shaman. So in the West we have always had a shamanic culture even if little evidence of it remains in existence. As such, all I am doing here in the 21st century is tapping back in to what my own ancestors would have been doing wherever they were from.

In this lifetime, I actually have no real idea of where my ancestors were from. I know where my grandparents and parents were born and have stories from childhood about my ancestors, tales passed down by the fire as it were, but my family's records have all but disappeared. Tracing them has so far proved impossible. To compound this I now live in a country that is not the one of my own birth. I have never felt any real connection to any particular culture, yet I still practice shamanism and I consider what I do to be authentic.

I did once, some time ago, look at training with another shaman as I felt that my own skills were less because I couldn't tie them to any one culture, nor had I been trained in shamanism by anyone in this reality. However, when I was told by this person that I had to accept that none of what I did had any value, I realised that it was just as valued as anything any human might give me, if not more so, as I had received it directly from my own spirit guides and allies. Why should it be any less? It was a good lesson to learn early on as it turned out. Sometimes you just have to believe in yourself, in what you do and the authenticity of it. When I look at others who practice shamanism today I see many across the world who have also been taught by their spirit guides and allies. This is becoming more and more common and perhaps is the way that shamans are being trained in the 21st century. It is a way to provide the world with authentic shamanism when we no longer live in tribal groups and so cannot receive our training within them.

My first steps on what I now know to be a shamanic path were very slow and tentative. My initial introduction was a completely unexpected and unasked for shamanic journey, where I met someone who I recognised immediately as my grandfather from a past life and who I now know as one of my guides. With him I learnt how to walk with consciousness through woods, how to work with plants and how to make offerings to spirits. At the time I didn't recognise this for what it was and by the time I did and had a name for it I realised I had actually been there for a long time.

I have always been stubborn and resistant to doing anything unless it is on my own terms and in my own way though, so looking back can see how I resisted acknowledging the path for a long time. It didn't feel as though it had been of my choosing in any way, but something that was being thrust upon me. My guides, however, were tenacious, patient and chipped away slowly at my resistance until there was no choice for me but to accept where I was and where I was being led.

The fact that I am taught by my guides and allies in spirit actually suits me, but although an amazing and interesting experience it isn't easy. It can be unnerving, frustrating as well as supportive, but it is completely authentic. There is no one on a power trip or telling me their way is better than someone else's, there is nothing except a genuine desire to teach, assist and support me however and wherever I need it. As I have needed to learn, so a situation has arisen where it has been possible for me to do so. I learn as they teach and then put it into practice and so gradually my shamanic path has unfolded before me.

I now live in Ireland and am what is called a 'blow in' i.e. someone who was not born here. Although Pagan at its ancestral roots, Catholicism is still the dominant belief system here. Although it is not as all controlling as it was, where I live the Church remains strong. Yet it is here that I found myself on this path and so believe that this, for now anyway, is where I need to be, to work and where my community is to be found.

My guides are also not Celtic, nor is the shamanism I practice. In fact my shamanism still doesn't link to any particular culture, but this no longer concerns me. As I am taught by my guides I may learn something that links to the culture they are from, for example early on, my Native American guide taught me how to make an offering to bird spirits with sage and feathers. This doesn't make my shamanism Native American in any way though, especially as I make my own sage bundles from the sage I have growing in my garden, working with the spirit of that which is native to where I live. Alongside this I have a strong connection with Lake Titicaca in Peru and when visiting there have had some very profound experiences and teaching from my tutelary spirits in non-ordinary reality, but again this does not mean that I practice South American or Andean shamanism.

My shamanism is both part of who I am and where I am. When I work with the land I connect with the spirits of the place, in ritual I connect with the spirits of the place and the energy of those present and I allow myself to be guided by them as well as by my own guides and allies. When I work with others in healing I do exactly the same.

One of the underlying beliefs in shamanism is that everything that exists has its own energy. For me this means that everything that exists has its own consciousness on some level and we are all connected. By tapping in to this energy and consciousness I have access to a wide range of energy, support, learning and guidance at all times. I have learnt to watch for signs and omens as I move through the day and spend much of my waking hours 'walking the line', one foot in this reality, one in non-ordinary reality in order to work with the guidance and messages that are all around me. This interconnectedness means that everything that exists needs to be treated with respect, which is why when I am working or carrying out ritual I always connect with the spirits of the place to ask permission and to ascertain their needs before doing so. I then ensure I carry out their wishes. It doesn't matter to me if I am in my own garden, a stone circle, forest, my healing room, someone's home or another country; the underlying principle for me remains the same.

A few years ago I was asked to perform a ritual in a stone circle. I visited the stones on my own prior to working there with the group. I met the spirits of the stones and learnt what they required of me if I was to work there. Part of this was to thank the stones once our work was complete. On the evening I returned with the group the sea mist had rolled in and as night fell the mist became more and more dense. By the time the ritual was complete it was actually raining. In our hurry to collect up our drums and protect them and their spirits from the rain I somehow forgot to thank the stones, despite offerings being made to them by the others. In bed that night, just as I was dropping off to sleep I remembered this. Immediately wide awake I knew I needed to rectify the situation immediately and so journeyed to Otherworld to meet with the spirits of the stones so that I could offer my thanks and fulfil the agreement I had made with them.

Like so many others I work alone, as a solitary practitioner. This doesn't mean that I don't have a community, but that I do not practice my shamanism with a partner or in a group. Perhaps because of where I live, I work quietly and unobtrusively, I don't force my beliefs on others, nor they on me. I don't shout about what I do but nor do I hide it. I live on the edge of a village and have a community with which I work. It is a loose one consisting of those who need my help for healing or teaching, some of my community are local, some are not. Sometimes my community is large, at other times small and, like most things in life, it ebbs and flows. Those who need me always seem to find me somehow.

For me a large part of being authentic is to be myself whether I am working as a healer, performing ritual or just going about my daily life. I do not own robes, wear a mask, feathers or anything else that some might expect someone working with shamanism to wear. I believe it is important to be honest and for me this means that what you see is what you get, were I to be any other way it would seem like smoke and mirrors and would not be authentic for me. In my healing room I have tools; drums, rattles, crystals, feathers, sage, flower essences, bells, chimes, stones and singing bowls. While I have these and love working with the spirits of them, they are not essential to my work. I have heard of those who have refused to perform healing or ritual because they do not have their tools with them. For me this makes no sense at all. If I am a 'hollow bone', journey and connect with my guides and allies, they will work with me, through me and thus I will always have access to all I need. This is a belief that I hold strong. The only time I would refuse to work would be if it felt wrong, if I felt that I or anyone else was at risk in any way or if something seemed beyond my ability.

Sometimes when I am travelling I am lucky enough to meet shamans from other cultures. One such meeting took place in Madagascar with the local witchdoctor. Throughout our time together we shared explanations of how we both worked. He told me that he worked with the spirits of his ancestors and so understood immediately when I said that I too worked with spirit helpers although not those of my blood ancestors. We also discovered that we both used plants and stones in our healing by working with the spirits of them and as we shared, we found more and more similarities in the ways we both worked. At one point the witchdoctor seemed puzzled and explained that he knew he did Malagasy magic, but he couldn't understand that what I did was also Malagasy magic, but that I wasn't Malagasy.

It struck me then that this was the first time I had really travelled to such an isolated part of the world and met someone who only had knowledge of their own culture and beliefs. The witchdoctor had no experience or reference points outside his own culture, nothing to relate what I did to, other than Malagasy magic and no concept that all around the world were others working in such similar ways, all of us following our own paths in shamanism and all of us completely authentic.

Living as a Heathen in 21st Century Britain

By Pete Jennings

For me personally, life is so much easier now as a Heathen than when I first started to become active in the 1980s. Due to the concerted efforts over the past five decades of a multitude of Pagan spiritual paths and organisations (including the Pagan Federation of which I was President), the media are in general better informed and less likely to label us as devil worshipers sacrificing babies and virgins and so on than they were back in the bad old days of lurid tabloid headlines. I am now less likely to have to explain what we are, and more likely to be asked onto radio and TV shows to give balance to fundamentalist rhetoric.

The UK Government recognises earth-centred spiritual paths and pays some of us to provide a Home Office chaplaincy service into prisons. Some of us are involved in interfaith dialogue with other religions. This is still a controversial idea to many, but I believe that talking and gaining understanding of each other is preferable to ignorance and fighting. Some Heathens do not associate themselves with Pagans, but I continue to enjoy intra-faith activities with Druids, Shamans, and Witches etc., sharing their conferences, magazines, camps and moots. Personally I feel that we have more in common than that which divides us.

Yet, it is not all mead and honeycakes. Some folk are still subject to discrimination and abuse within their family, community or even at work (despite the Equality Act 2010 making the latter illegal). One of the ways in which I and the Heathen and Pagan communities have tried to have their presence better officially recognised is by getting the official Census for the various countries within the United Kingdom to include or count Pagan and Heathen categories under religion, then encourage people to record them. Inevitably, some still fear their anonymity will be compromised while others label themselves so finitely as to be counted within a unique class of one.

A partial solution for this has been to persuade people to label themselves Pagan – Wiccan, Pagan – Druid or Pagan – Heathen etc., yet such is the individualistic nature of many even this was disagreed with. Some Heathens do not accept that theirs is a subdivision of the more general Pagan term, unlike Christians or Muslims who are willing to be classed as 'Christian – Baptist' or 'Muslim – Sunni' etc. However, even with those sorts of restrictions on getting an accurate count, there were more than 80,000 Pagan-related individuals counted in the 2011 England & Wales Census, about double the number reported a decade before. Estimates of the true figure range from 100,000 upwards, meaning that there are more of us than Buddhists, for example, who have always been a minority group recognised by the Government. Yet we continue be a divided group, often suspicious of leaders, organisations and writers within our community, and governmental organisations outside it. This does not serve us well, and often hinders the progress made on the 'divided we fall' principle. A leader who I took over from said it was 'like herding cats' and that still rings true to me.

When I first started reading about Paganism in the 1970s the choice was very limited: a few good witchcraft books sold from beneath the counter of certain shops like illicit pornography, or sensationalist fiction such as Dennis Wheatley. There was next to no material on paths other than the most popular witchcraft in its many forms. Some books eventually started to filter through from the USA, but were inevitably orientated for that country and often quite simplistic. Eventually the UK started to get its own literary act together. Still most of the books were beginners' guides (albeit including Druidry, Odinism and Shamanism) but as an avid reader I got fed up with the same old material being recycled.

Of course, from a publishing point of view, beginners' books sell best (and I have written some myself), but eventually there was enough of an experienced audience to justify better researched, more advanced studies. I applaud the academic Professor Ronald Hutton for showing people how it could be done, citing proper references for every statement made and going back to source materials to challenge our own 'sacred cows'.

This new wave of books has enhanced the qualities of talks and discussions within our community, and now includes many books concentrating on specifically narrow interests to deal with them in detail. I particularly enjoy writing in that way now. Since I research and write principally for my own interest, whatever follows in book sales or talks are a bonus.

The biggest difference of all to my life as a modern Heathen in my sixties is the internet. It did not really exist when I took my first tentative steps in trying to find others of a like mind. Using pseudonyms to prevent identification by work colleagues or journalists, and moots not yet being invented, it was extremely difficult, particularly outside major cities. Any debates tended to be via slow mail letters or expensive landline telephone calls. Mobile phones were not yet generally available either.

Now I can communicate by email or web forum every day across the world cheaply and easily, and access most original texts I want to research from the comfort of my own office. Of course it does have the downside that instant communication can lack forethought in posting things better left unsaid, and rumours can spread out of control. (I did not die in 2005 – that Peter Jennings was the anchor man for ABC News in the USA!)

Conferences and camps have proliferated too: from the couple of small ones in London in the 1980s we are now spoilt for choice, with at least one in almost every county of England and some reaching audiences counted in thousands. As a rural dweller I love the chance to meet others of a similar ilk and trade ideas and experiences. Otherwise, my path could become a lonely one without fresh stimulus to re-energise it. Those events have inevitably become more professionally run, with a better range and quality of speakers and workshops than their early forbears and I spend a lot of time and energy travelling around to them each year.

Yet, as I look at all the developments I have seen over the past 40 years, they are as nothing if I have not developed my own insight, ability, faith, connectedness or whatever. I am a human like any other, so will inevitably fall short of my ideals, but it has been said that no spiritual path has value unless it changes the thoughts and actions of its followers. Embracing what was once termed Odinism or Asatru, or more latterly Heathenry, has had several really visible effects on me:

I stopped working in sales and sought out more meaningful, moral, honest and hopefully more socially helpful employment. In my case that involved studying first as a counsellor/ psychotherapist and more latterly as a social worker. I developed my interest in history and as a result became an enthusiastic Anglo-Saxon and Viking re-enactor. This has enabled me to get a taste of the cultures in which my beliefs are rooted, and pass on my knowledge to the public.

As someone not afraid to live openly as a Heathen, I was encouraged to write articles, then books and lectures. Everyone has something to offer back as a gift to their Gods and Goddesses, and I like to think that my previous abilities as an organiser, entertainer, folklorist, radio presenter etc. have been utilised by my deities to increase their visibility.

Of course, my path has introduced me to many wonderful people, who form the bulk of my friends. They are very different to the people I once associated with. I am fortunate also that my wife is of a similar path, which gives us some major interests to take joy in together. To non-Pagans I guess I appear as a slightly eccentric, larger-than-life, gruffly independent individual who is not afraid to speak his mind.

At a practical level I tend to support environmentally friendly causes and energy sources, try to shop ethically and locally and act in an honest and straightforward way. That does not necessarily mean that I am a 'good' man, but only that I try to be and in that I sometimes fail. It also means that I spend far more time than I ought to on the computer as well as buying and reading loads of books, and I can get quite irate when I see situations that are unfair.

I can look back to my early writings and notes and see how heavily I was influenced by the then dominant Wiccan methods and ideas. Since then, through combined research and modern translations we now have a far better idea of what Heathens historically got up to, and what they believed in. Hence I have developed a ritual style that incorporates some of those ancient practices when useful, yet acknowledges new methods may be more appropriate for the very different culture I live in today.

I am optimistic for the future of Heathens and Pagans in general in the UK, but know that now we are better established we make a bigger, more important target for religious fundamentalists. Both our biggest strength and weakness is our diversity, but I would not have it any other way. As a path that demands that we think for ourselves and establish our own truths we will never have the mass appeal of highly organised religions with powerful officials and texts giving absolute answers on a plate. Nor should we ever seek that mass appeal, but remain a group with divergent ideas that thinking people sometimes find useful for themselves.

Memoirs of Sacred Purpose

By Hilde Liesens

Just at the right moment, the cloud lifted. With magical timing, the landscape of lights below us was revealed. From the top of Moel Famau, we could see all the way to Wrexham, Chester and Liverpool: the western corner of the Bowland Shale gas field.

Every New Year's Eve random people push a wheelbarrow of logs up Moel Famau, the tallest hill in the Clwydian Range. It's not a Pagan event. It's not even organised. But with some unconscious Pagan instinct a couple of hundred people trudge up that tall hill in the middle of the night in winter to call back the light with a bonfire and some fireworks.

Six members of The Warrior's Call, Pagans United Against Fracking, climbed with them that night. We took a log to add to the communal fire, a small sacrifice for the returning Sun. We carried flasks with mulled wine and hot tea. At the summit, we counted in 2015 and watched as flares were set off, turning the low cloud that covered the hilltop a glowing red.

But Paul, one of our group, had something else planned. After toasting the New Year, he drew us aside for a brief ceremony. In wind so strong it threatened to throw us off our feet, he called peace to the quarters and welcomed the elements. Then he started a prayer, calling on the spirits and gods of the land below, confirming his and our promise to protect it.

At that exact moment, with all the force of magic, the cloud moved off the hilltop and showed us what he was praying about. We saw a wide landscape of lights: Wrexham and Chester, Liverpool, where Underground Coal Gasification (UCG) is proposed, with Manchester and Blackpool in the far distance. Promising to do all we could to prevent gas flares from being added to the clusters of lights below, we all felt the emotion of the moment.

I barely knew what fracking was when Tim asked me if I wanted to be involved in a public ritual at Glastonbury to protect the land from it. I had read an article in the Guardian that pointed out that exploiting new fossil fuel reserves is a bad idea if we are to limit global warming to two degrees centigrade.

Climate change and the effect it has on the Earth's biosphere is a cause close to my heart. Because of it, I have radically changed my lifestyle over the past few years. My husband and I have embarked on a thorough house renovation that will drastically reduce our carbon footprint. The shale gas drive goes against all that I stand for. It is the front line of climate change in the UK. So with the Glastonbury ritual coming up, I started reading more.

For fracking to have any meaningful impact on our energy supply, we would need thousands of fracking pads all across the country. The infrastructure for each requires a plot the size of a couple of football pitches to be cleared of vegetation and concreted over.

And then the lorries start arriving. It comes down to 200 lorries making return journeys through small towns and villages, and along narrow country lanes that are not built for that kind of traffic. The noise and traffic disruption are considerable, and change the character of the area.

That is just the logistics at the periphery. The actual technology of hydraulic fracturing, or fracking for short, is another story. Water mixed with a cocktail of chemicals and sand is pumped into the earth at high pressure to fracture the rock and release the gas. As a Pagan woman, I can't help thinking of this as a rape of the Mother. The idea makes me cringe. It just feels wrong.

Experience in Australia and America has shown that the technology has a number of destructive effects on the local environment. Around a fracking site, nothing is safe. Flares burning off excess gas make a hellish noise and pollute the air. The cocktail of water and chemicals is more contaminated when it comes back out of the well, carrying naturally occurring radioactive materials up with it. The concrete the wells are cased with inevitably cracks over time, causing leaks. The interference with the geology causes earth tremors.

People who live near established fracking wells in the US and Australia report breathing difficulties, skin conditions, and increased still births in animals as well as in humans. It seems obvious that, in a densely populated country like England, these effects could be widespread and devastating.

The aspect of this that really makes me see red is the intimate relationship that exists between the fracking industry and Government. Lord Brown, to mention one example, is a member of the House of Lords and also the chairman of Cuadrilla, the shale gas drilling company. He was appointed as Government Lead Non-Executive in June 2010. He works with Secretaries of State to appoint non-executives to the board of each Government department.

Is it too farfetched to imagine that he would have appointed people to the Department of Energy and Climate Change who are sympathetic to his business? And shouldn't there be a law against such conflicts of interest?

None of us had anticipated the success of that first ritual in Glastonbury. Tim put out The Warrior's Call and it was answered in overwhelming numbers. The Facebook event went viral. In the weeks leading up to our ceremony, thousands of people across the world clicked the 'Attending' button.

On that day in September 2013, about 300 people attended the ritual at the foot of Glastonbury Tor. Simultaneously, other rituals tuned in with ours, creating a web of protection from Australia to Argentina and from Sweden to South-Africa. It was a magical day, filled with synchronicities and moments of power. We used the Warrior's Sigil, especially designed for the occasion, to focus the intent of all those rituals.

In Pagan communities, that ritual raised a lot of awareness about fracking in the UK and around the world. The Warrior's Sigil has become a symbol of power for Pagans protecting the land. It is flown on banners at protection camps such as Upton, near Chester, and had a big presence at the mega-blockade in Bentley, Australia. A number of people have it tattooed on their bodies. It is recognised across the world.

There obviously was a hunger to link engagement in the anti-fracking movement with our Pagan spirituality. Pagans have a strong spiritual and emotional bond with the land they hold sacred. We tend to be genuinely concerned about large-scale issues such as climate change, but when actual trees are being cut down, our waterways are in danger of being contaminated, and our land is directly threatened, we get actively involved to defend it.

Having tapped into that energy, we were not just going to let it dissipate. The core group that visioned and performed the Glastonbury ritual has kept working together. Our aim is to inspire and empower Pagans in the UK and beyond to get involved in the anti-fracking groups in their areas. We've organised many events to keep our momentum going.

We have kept the Call alive with two more worldwide rituals. Our inaugural ritual worked with the element of Air, stretching a web of protection all across the world. Six months later, we worked with Water, sending our blessings down waterways to meet in the oceans to heal and protect the element most threatened by fracking. Earth Web, a year after the original ritual, worked with stones, creating points of power in the landscape that people can return to and access when the going gets tough.

We go out to speak to Pagans face to face. Early in 2014, we held talks for Pagan moots in South Wales. The talks led up to our first Morrigan Encampment in the spring. These events inspired people to take their own initiatives and become involved in protest camps.

Melanie from South Wales organised a summer weekend festival, and regularly drives the length of Wales to lend support to the Borras & Holt protection camp. She had never attempted anything like it in her life, but she heard The Warrior's Call and answered it wholeheartedly. Paul has been instrumental in founding Frack Free Dee and does everything he can to support the camp at Upton while working a full-time job of night shifts.

These people are the heroes of our movement. They loudly deny that they are in any way special. They're just doing what needs to be done. It is obvious, though, that they have overcome many of the barriers we all face: our time is precious, our families need our energy and attention, our jobs sap our enthusiasm. But they have found the courage to get stuck in regardless.

So what is it that gives these people the strength to do what they do?

First and most importantly, they are connected to a supportive community, often more than one. They are well integrated into the local anti-fracking movement and have made friends there. They also have strong links to their Pagan communities. They have a spiritual practice of their own, finding support in the world of Spirit.

With the money we have made from generous donations, selling merchandise, and fundraising initiatives, we aim to give Pagans the knowledge and support they need to take the plunge and get stuck in.

Our Morrigan Encampments bring Pagans together in community, widening and deepening their network. They learn the strategies they need to build a community campaign and take effective action on the front line. They also find a healing space where people get a chance to work ritually with their love of the land and their sorrow of it being desecrated.

After just 18 months, we have achieved a lot with The

Warrior's Call. In the year to come, we will go out to meet many more Pagans in their local areas. We are specifically working on growing our movement and getting more people involved in organising our events and activities. With more people, we will also be able to help Pagans who are involved in community campaigns and protection camps with knowledge, resources, and spiritual support.

In every corner of the country, fracking companies are opposed by local communities. Local government often is on the side of the people and rejects their planning applications. The fracking companies then appeal directly to Government, and have their application forced through regardless.

As time goes by, more and more sites will need protecting. The movement will need more people on the ground all over the country. As Pagans who revere the land, we can't contemplate gas flares burning across the landscape, marking the places where the Earth has been cracked open. The Warrior's Call sounds for everyone to hear. How will you answer it?

Druid Living

By Adele Sutcliffe

It's taken a long time for me to finally find my path, but this last year I think I have. I have always thought I was Wiccan and followed that path, from being a very young girl in the early 1970s. Having to go out in the dark to the local shop to get my stepfather some cigarettes, I always thought that the witches would come and get me if I didn't ask for their guidance to get me to the shop and back safe. Upon getting into bed that night I would then thank them for that. Way back then there was no internet and no books available to me. It wasn't until later on that a friend of a friend pointed out to me the Wiccan path, so in a way I have always followed it.

The years went by, I got married, had a family, got divorced, got married for a second time, and found my path again. Looking back I know I had to put it to one side for a while and deeply regret that.

About 12 years ago I met a woman who I really didn't know and she spoke to me about the Wiccan path. It was just out of the blue, I had never revealed my path to anyone and for this person to know was, to me, rather strange, but I allowed her to carry on; that in turn got me back onto my path again. Slowly I gathered the things that at the time thought I needed: wand, athame, God figure, Goddess figure, offering bowls etc, all from a shop in my local town. I gathered the books from the internet and bookshops. This was the path I followed for a long while.

I was then put onto a book by an American man called Scott Cunningham. I found a copy of his book *Wicca: A Guide for the Solitary Practitioner*. Well, needless to say, that got me hooked, not on the path of Wicca, but witchcraft. I at first thought they were the same until I dug deeper. I was then told that witchcraft was more based on the old ways, looking for herbs, healing and cleansing. After about a year and a half, my husband decided to do a Druid course, which involved learning about Druidry every month for a year. Lessons were sent each month, with work to be done and sent back. Before he had finished the course I had signed up for it too, not really knowing what I had let myself in for. Not only that, I had signed up for a Kitchen Witch course too. I knew this was going to keep me busy and it has.

They both started in June, although I had done two lessons in the Kitchen Witch course by the time the Druid course started. Both, in their own way, have shown me another path that I already follow, the Kitchen Witch course has shown me a deeper understanding of working with herbs, crystals and deities. Even though I had my Goddess and God, I knew there were others, but not as many as I had discovered. I have learnt a greater understanding of them.

I was always interested in herbs and took this course to learn about ones I hadn't worked with; the same applied to the crystals. It was a fabulous course and I would recommend it to anyone.

The Druid course took me in another direction. There are three paths, Druid, Ovate and Bard. Slowly after a couple of months it became very clear to me and to my tutor which path I was on; I'm Ovate. Now, I never tell people my path, but those who know me have asked and I have revealed. I am very happy on this newly discovered path. Some would say I was always on it, but needed this for me to realise it. Others would say it is newly found. Either way I'm happy. I get up each day and thank my Goddess for the things I have. Looking outside, I always get excited that there are squirrels in the trees playing chase. The birds come to my feeder, one is cheeky and taps on the window as if to say hello.

My Awen is flowing well, I have so many ideas for paintings, cooking, and baking. I am grateful for this year's bounty of fruits which I am able to gather to make pies and jams for the winter ahead.

Just back from Glastonbury, I felt I was being torn in so many different directions. It was awful to feel drained in such a beautiful place, but not to let it get to me, I went on a walk and met a lovely man who also showed me that I could live of the land as well, if I know what to eat. He told me that hawthorn leaves and berries were edible in small amounts, something I didn't know. I ate sloe berries and beech nuts and just sat in the woods gathering in the beauty of my world. This is a place I am more at home with than anywhere else, just sitting in a wood, watching the world go by. Think how many of my ancestors have walked this path before me, and how many will walk after me? I love foraging in woodlands collecting the conkers for my altar along with the leaves that have fallen and acorns, eating blackberries along the way. Coming home, it's nice to see what I have in my small patio garden and what I can gather to put into pots for next year. I was lucky enough to be able to get some lavender from Chalice Well Gardens, in Glastonbury. I spoke to the gardener and he said I could take a bit of what I needed. He gave the secateurs to cut the lavender and allowed me to take one or two stems from a couple of herbs he was growing. I feel very honoured.

Educating Hampshire – One Woman's Attempts to 'Normalise' Paganism

By Arietta Bryant

It is October 31st 2014. This morning my 'tween daughter announced to me that this year she would be 'trick-or-treating as a *zombie nerd*' and gave me a list of items that she simply could not do without to make her costume perfect. As is normal, in our household of shift-working parents and slightly oddball children, we were already behind on our Samhain preparations. No pumpkin had been purchased, no decorations hung and I was about three weeks behind on the household chores. But I was determined that this year, one of the first where I have not been busy organising a public Samhain ceremony, I would set a good example to my kids and we would have a lovely family ritual at home, after the obligatory trick-or-treating had gone on. However, this was not to be.

Dragging my hubby along with me (still more zombie than human himself having got home from work at 6am) we braved the large town centre shopping mall. Several shops were decked out in fake cobwebs and cardboard pumpkins, staff (some more willingly than others) sported various levels of costuming and spooky sound effects could be heard in several establishments. But nowhere could we find a single vial of fake blood or other gory makeup accessory.

This was not because our town has anything against Halloween (or Samhain). The shops had contained plenty of our desired items up to this point, but it seems that something slightly unsettling had occurred in the night preceding October 31st, when all of the spooky items, plastic bats and rubber noses had been locked back away in the stock room to make space for tinsel, baubles, and Santa hats!

We came home empty handed and I made the best of it with some red lipstick for my daughter's zombie look. We lit candles in the window instead of carving a Jack-o-lantern and the kids collapsed in a sugar coma after a pretty successful raid of the neighbours' candy jars.

Later that night I sat in front of my altar and lit candles in remembrance of those in my circle of friends who had passed away and I left gifts of cake and ale as a libation for the spirits before heading up to bed.

Sleep, though, would not come as I was plagued by the images of a sales assistant dressed as a traditional Halloween witch selling nothing but Santa hats. I just wanted to scream at them, to explain that the corporate desire to make cash from our obsessive and impulsive overspending at Christmas is whitewashing one of the most important holidays in the Pagan calendar: Samhain.

But as Pagans we don't speak up for what we believe in and I feel that is really sad. All this was highlighted further by a chance encounter with another family while we were out trick or treating. The family had stopped us in the street and said, 'Here is something for you. No tricks, just a treat.' They handed each of my children a small bag and went on their way. The bag turned out to contain kid-friendly literature about the teachings of the Bible as well as a few boiled sweets. This 'Christian gift' might well have made some people angry (I can hear it already 'Proselytising Christians, out to spoil everyone's fun...') but I just felt frustrated. These people had taken the time to try to pass on a message to people, but I had just bowed out of the sacred part of this day and had to settle for a watered down, last-minute, version of it, which might as well be renamed Costume & Candy Day.

I pledged that night to do everything in my power to find the magic which is missing from our festival and to spread it around. To that end, my daughter and I have considered taking small votive candles with perhaps small information slips attached, and trading them for the 'treats' at each house we visit. We will leave them with the gift of light, and the gift of knowledge.

It seems I may have stumbled upon something of a 'calling'...

Being the Pagan equivalent of *Little Britain's* 'Only Gay in the Village', I have always considered myself to be very much out of the broom closet and have always been willing to answer questions about my, often misunderstood, beliefs. Well another chance has shown itself to continue this education.

I work in a secondary school where staff and students are planning to take part in 'Christmas Jumper Day'. It is all for charity and I certainly don't begrudge them doing it. In addition, in a wonderfully inclusive move, the headteacher has also opened the day to those who do not celebrate Christmas, by offering them the option of coming to school dressed in their own religion's ceremonial garments.

And so I pondered the idea... Should I come into my place of work in my robe? What would I gain? What did I have to lose? Sure, I could be laughed at and not taken seriously, but would that be any worse than wearing a dodgy Crimbo sweater? I spent a couple of days pondering this and eventually came around to the idea that I should put my money where my mouth is, therefore if I am going to be an out and proud Pagan Priestess then why the heck shouldn't I wear my robe and headdress one day a year for work? After all it is for charity!

I would like more Pagans to feel free to be open about their spirituality. I firmly believe that the more public we become and the more we are willing to answer people's questions, then the more normalised Paganism will become. Eventually, saying that you are a Pagan will no more raise an eyebrow than if you say you are a Christian.

The holiday season is a time for all faiths to cheer ourselves through the dark of winter and to welcome in the growing light. We should be free to express those celebrations publicly!

Druidry in Action

By Mark Rosher

This week I…how to finish that sentence in a form that presents Druidry in Action on a 'Pagan Planet'? Because for me the word Druid is as much a verb as a noun or a title. Indeed, if one isn't 'doing' Druidry then what is the worth of the word? When you examine it closely, your life is simply you being you, doing what you do. So are the labels we tie to ourselves adding meaning or confusion? Paganism encompasses such a breadth of practice it can be hard to determine what is and what is not part of it. As someone who, for want of a better label, offers the word Druid when asked for a spiritual, religious, or practical description, my life choices are informed by the relationships I build or notice in the natural world. To tie it tighter about me, let's call them relationships of landscape, heritage and creativity; or mud, blood and magic. But if you want to imagine me the Druid, look far away from the robed ritualist of tradition stood in a stone circle, for I'm more likely striding the hilltop in stout walking boots, or digging over the garden dodging errant chickens.

My practice is deeply bound to pragmatism, indeed one could call my path one of Pragmatic Druidry. Until recently I was fully employed in the energy transmission industry – not one where Druids might be expected! And yet even amidst high voltages and oil containments there are places where the spirit of the land calls; admittedly it often calls for help. But if in my daily, quite technical, work I can gently engineer movement that lowers the impact of our presence in the landscape, if I can inculcate a little understanding of the land as a living conglomeration of entities, if I can calm in part the emotional hurt we ever-burgeoning humans place on the life of the planet, Druidry is done. Working within my geographic community, and chairing a parish council,

Druidry continues. Fostering better community relations. Seeking to mitigate the hurt to the local landscape inherent in meeting the needs of a growing population. Making space available for human to meet wildlife in ways non-detrimental to that wildlife; protecting a field, a tree, a river… It's not easy in the countering thrust of commercial profit-driven organisations that are focused entirely on turning what you have into what they want. It's an unending battle. Most often, they win. Sometimes, 'we' do. In fact, ignoring the personal calls of my animist perception, of welcoming the sunrise and speaking to the non-human life one encounters, my only wholly Druid work is co-holding an intangible space in which others find Druidry. I am a trustee of The Druid Network, a registered charity in England and Wales based mainly on the internet with a remit to inform, inspire and facilitate Druidry as a religious practice.

Druidry informs me, though, in the way I live – negotiating my potential personal impact on the planet with the planet, but not to the point I am puritanically uncomfortable. It provokes me to explore ways of living; for example driving a hybrid car, but seeking to reduce my reliance upon it; installing a solar roof while being aware that demand reduction is more important than additional generation; growing more food in my garden even as I understand most people cannot, even as I understand I cannot, even grow enough just for one. Druidry informs me when I buy locally and organically. Druidry informs me when I holiday on my island rather than abroad. And yes, there is ritual on hilltop and riverside. But I am relating to this world, not seeking to ascend beyond it; speaking to the gods in the land, not to one set above it. And yes I do use entertainment electronics, I do take trips overseas, I do ride a motorbike for pleasure…does the good mitigate the not-so-good? It's impossible to say, but perhaps in these short paragraphs I've identified a Pagan Druidry less bound up in robes and ritual than is generally presumed.

Working with Tolkien

By Calantirniel

In my experience as a seeker, many alternative spiritual practitioners who were raised as Christians changed their personal belief system toward a more nature-based choice – *not* because of an adversity to the Christ consciousness on its own. Their distaste is instead directed toward the typical religious structures in place – basically, 'the Church'. In ideal circumstances, they often loved the support the community provided, but not at the emotional cost of inflicting fear, guilt and other oppressive means used by many of these organisations to keep people in line while discouraging them from thinking for themselves. When conditions were not ideal, sometimes the community and even family support were diminished or even absent (and in the worst cases, abuse was present as well).

In the past, Pagans who wanted to integrate the Christ energy into their natural path were heavily discouraged. After all, we can look at the many world mythologies that do not align and in fact directly oppose the Christian-aligned ethical and/or moral choices. Socially, especially in the USA, both Pagans and Christians often encourage these spiritual choices to remain separate, perhaps to strengthen their identity and perpetuate the concept of 'us versus them'. However, if a relationship has been balanced and lovingly achieved with the Christ, while fully understanding the need for our indigenous stories from all cultures, what can be done? Many good solutions exist; the most prevalent being to understand the core of the ancient stories and apply love while releasing fear in our spiritual and living decisions and practices as much as we can.

However, some have found another solution. There exists a deep and stirring mythology that does not conflict with the

Christian paradigm (the Bible). It is found in the most unlikely of places, but the discovery can be like finding the spiritual waters that thoroughly quench your soul's thirst. Many know of this mythos already, but never looked deeper since it is presented as fiction – and let's face it, all stories, especially the ancient ones are fiction, right? Yet we obtain the truth in no better way than through telling stories. The truth is not the same thing as fact, as even facts can be woven into an untruth. The truth is something we understand at our very core, whether we can explain it or not – we feel it! We know it!

So, what is this solution, this cosmology? Oddly, for those with whom this resonates, it is found in the Middle-Earth stories, especially of the Elven viewpoint, that were brought to us by Professor JRR Tolkien (collectively called the Legendarium). Quite particularly, it is in the posthumously-published Elven origin stories, which include *The Silmarillion*.

If you find you do not resonate with these stories, you can stop reading here. However, if you find that you have a strong and positive pull in your energy toward these stories, I invite you to investigate further and implement these cosmologies where it seems comfortable, whether you are Christian, Pagan or both – or neither.

While some would have you believe Tolkien made these stories up entirely in his head, research has been revealed that shows this is not necessarily the case. Dr Corey Olsen of Mythgard Institute (www.tolkienprofessor.com) shows a history lesson regarding the Inklings, which consisted of Tolkien, C.S. Lewis and other writers. When in regular meetings, the Inklings often reviewed each others' work to improve their storytelling and writing skills. When Tolkien's stories were discussed, the others in the group were excited about the material and wanted to know more details. Now, if Tolkien had indeed made the stories up himself, his response would be different than the one he had. He instead told them when seeking further details of his stories, paraphrased as, 'I will go find out.'

In a 1967 interview on British radio, Tolkien was quite talkative about his popular Middle-Earth stories in print at the time (*The Hobbit* and *Lord of the Rings*) when the host asked him if he worshipped the Valar, the beings of power, which was more defined by 1973 in *The Silmarillion,* but not well-known to most readers at the time. It was strange to then witness a long pause of utter silence – so much that the radio host embarrassingly retracted his question, which then prompted Tolkien to provide this response – that he is a devout, practicing Catholic. He left it there, never answering yes or no to the original question. The remainder of the interview was conducted on a lighter note, with Tolkien being as talkative as he had been for most of the interview. It leaves the listener thinking, why would Tolkien do this?

He also left behind other subtle clues, including artwork early on that showed how he entered (in his perception) what can be termed as the Imaginal Realm to witness and even retrieve his wondrous experiences. Because he mastered ancient and modern languages better than anyone else in the last century at least, and he had access to many ancient materials being an Oxford University linguistic professor, perhaps he could more deeply understand and remember his experiences in this state and bring them forth as story. He began this process in 1917, decades prior to publishing his well-known stories. He continued to perfect his understanding by changing parts of his extensive notes he kept, which after his death allowed his son Christopher to publish not just *The Silmarillion,* but also the 12-volume set called the *History of Middle-Earth,* as well as *The Unfinished Tales.*

Luckily, proof does not matter to those who are touched very deeply by the Legendarium. It is a feeling that quite literally feels as if it is in your bones and DNA, and is experienced by some as singing. While many reputable spiritual seekers of various religious backgrounds explore the rather universal principals shown in Tolkien's life as well as the Legendarium and applying this resonance to existing spiritual pathways, the question then becomes: can the complexity and level of detail in the Legendarium itself provide a sole means of a complete spiritual pathway? In 2005, a small group of seekers from diverse Christian and Pagan backgrounds worldwide gathered together online to discover if this is indeed a viable possibility. The results? A definite affirmative!

If this is intriguing to you, please start with *The Silmarillion*. If you feel these stories deep within your soul, you are not alone. Find more resources at www.elvenspirituality.com.

Health/Illness

By Crystal Rainfeather

Spirituality has affected every aspect of my entire life, more so the past 13 years of being a witch, and to an even greater extent for the past eight years of being quite ill. I've never been the picture of perfect health, but now I live with heart failure (among other heart conditions), lower back issues (disc problems, sciatica), and signs of kidney dysfunction. Added to that has been a lack of healthcare, extreme financial hardships, and now a gravely ill mother.

I never thought about health problems as being anything more than obstacles and hardships, let alone that there was a *purpose* for them. Then again, I spent the majority of my life fearing death more than *anything* else. Through many losses, facing my own mortality and, ultimately, my spiritual path, I no longer have that fear because I finally realised I am part of an eternal cycle – the sacred Circle of life, death, and rebirth. Yes, our bodies die and return to the soil, but no soul is ever truly 'dead' because the essence lives on, finding new realms and new incarnations to continue its journey.

Paganism has made me acutely aware of a bigger picture, and how important it is to keep that in mind when everything else seems to fall apart. I am not the whole. My pains and tears are not those of everyone. But I *am* my own worst enemy. I *am* ego-driven and self-sabotaging. I *am* made of both light and dark. Being a witch has taught me some harsh realities about acknowledgement, responsibility, and balance... And that all of these things are never fully learned because there are countless variations. Are you familiar with the phrase, 'Go with the flow'? It's a cliché, but oh-so-true. I tend to cling, to be a creature of habit, and to resist relinquishing the notion of control, so being laid back and riding the currents of life is anything but easy... Another necessary 'lesson'? Yes, but it's one that has, admittedly, made me question the sense of humour of Deity and the Universe more than once over the past decade or two.

Nature Herself – our Mother, our sustainer, our global heartbeat – has an endless wellspring of beauty, grace, hope and teachings. The trick is to pay attention, to be 'present', and to *allow* ourselves to be open to the experience...to something greater. Even nature-related hobbies/passions such as bird watching, photography and journaling have kept me sane, grounded, thankful, compassionate, and filled with empathy. My love for all that is beyond my daily, often-difficult life, and for all that is mysterious, magical, and unknown, is what inspires, comforts, and restores me time and time again. Nature truly is the great healer, on every level. Our ancestors knew this, and we must come into this knowledge ourselves, in order to grow as spiritual beings.

If I were to narrow down a list of what my struggles and path have taught me, I'd have to have the fact that I am here to learn in the number 1 position. A close second would be that as both a fragile, flawed human, and a Divine being, I'm stronger and more resilient than I truly understand.

Employing the help of sporadic meditation, breathing exercises, gemstone energies, *and* helping others, has allowed me to find a plethora of coping tools. Each method is different and brings about assorted outcomes. Meditation, for example, often leads me to inner journeys and unexpected insights whereas the breathing techniques bring about calm. Gemstones (much like herbs, incense, candles...) can soothe, energise, uplift, allow release, etc., depending on the energy contained within the specific item. Healing rituals for the Earth, giving readings, offering counselling, working with totems and guides – all these activities redirect my energy into a specific, focused task and open up a time where my thoughts *and* actions are centred on others. This time, no matter how brief, can mean the difference between staying in a 'negative' state and allowing that hindering energy to dissipate and be replaced by more productive and soul-full energies.

Being a witch, a shaman, a nature lover, an eternal optimist, a student of all-there-is, and someone who follows her own intuition and path is at the core of my spiritual self. It is the *knowing who I am* that has allowed me to gain more than I have lost and to fight more than I retreat. After all, living with a serious, even life-threatening, illness isn't about a cure-all, or attaining a Zen-like state any more than it's about just accepting it and not doing all you can to see another day… It's about appreciating the journey, taking the good with the bad, being in touch with the Divine that is within you as well as all around, and finding (rather than losing) yourself along the way.

Re-Analysing the Wheel of the Year

By Frances Billinghurst

The seasonal Wheel of the Year is central to most Pagan paths today. Yet, despite this, there are still few alternatives offered beyond the traditional placements. For someone like myself who resides in the Southern Hemisphere, the advice to merely move sabbat dates around by six months rarely accurately reflects the seasons, especially within a country as large as Australia. Where I live, for example, the grain harvest occurs around midsummer, Samhain is often mild, and lambs tend to be born in the autumn to make use of the grass growth encouraged by the rains. This means that many of the associated sabbatical myths also do not fit. One solution is to observe the seasons of Australian Aboriginal people, and at first glance, this seems a logical and relatively easy task. In reality, however, it is not so especially when the different climate zones are taken into consider.

The Australian Aboriginals viewed that part of the land where they resided as 'country' and as such, each country had its own Dreaming stories that explained how things came into being. Each country also had its own seasonal calendar that was based around plant growth, the appearance of animals, and weather patterns. Where I live is Kaurna country and their calendar consists of six seasons:

Woltatti (November and December): The hot season. Movement to the coastal areas where food supplies are plentiful.

Bokarra (January and February): Hot north winds, stormy and tempestuous weather. Old grass is burnt to encourage new growth in the spring.

Parnatti (March and April): Autumn arrives with the

appearance of the 'Parna' star forecasting a change in the seasons and the need to move inland.

Wadlworngatti (May to July): Collect fruits, berries and seeds. Hunting of game and building more waterproof huts.

Kudilla (August and September): Winter, icy cold south westerly winds. Plains become marshy and swampy.

Wultutti (October and November): The appearance of the 'Wilti-Willo' star marks the time to move to the plains and hunt the game that has been attracted by the new grass growth.

Taking these observations in consideration is important as, over the years, the more I work with my local environment, a slightly different Wheel of the Year is emerging that allows me to acknowledge my European heritage and myths contained within the tradition I follow as well as the land upon which I reside and its traditional guardians. Some of the key points I currently work with are:

Winter Solstice (mid June): Rebirth of the Sun God is reflected in the eruption of brilliant yellow acacia flowers. Eucalypts shimmer as the deciduous imports have lost their leaves. The battle between the Holly and Oak Kings results in the Summer Oak King victorious.

Imbolc (August eve): Light is slowly returning to the land. However, winter still holds sway with unpredictable weather patterns. Spring rains encourage the abundance of growth as catkins and blossoms appear. Birds are restless as soon their young will hatch. Sightings of the allusive platypus can be spotted.

Spring Equinox (mid September): The Earth Bride wins against the Hag of Winter. The world has suddenly come alive and the promised abundance is on show. The deciduous trees are in leaf, the air contains the heady scent of blossom.

Bealtaine (November eve): The sacred union between the Lord of the Greenwood and the Queen of Life. The world erupts with abundance and opportunity, which is reflected in the chorus of cicadas.

Summer Solstice (mid December): Abundance of crops and harvest of grain. An element of urgency to get things completed before the heat arrives. The native gums pale in colour against the brilliant green of imported species. The battle between the Holly and Oak King takes place where the winter Holly King is the victor.

Lughnasadh (February eve): What fruit and grain has not been harvested is now the property of the Solar Death Goddess. The intense heat saps the life force from the land as the winter rains become a distant memory. Bush fires devastate the land yet assist in the regeneration of native plants, reflecting a life in death aspect.

Autumn Equinox (mid March): The headiness of the grape harvest as well as the fruit (particularly apples) hint towards the Inner Mysteries obtained through trance and intoxication. Between the autumn colour from the deciduous tree, the shadowy presence of the Dread Lord of Shadows is starting to be felt.

Samhain (May eve): Time of remembrance, reflection, and chance to tidy up loose ends. Fly agaric mushrooms reflect the delicate balance as the veils between the worlds apart. The rains return, quenching the thirsty land, and the Dread Lord of Shadows and his counterpart, the Hag of Winter, make their presence known as the air chills.

The 'traditional' Wheel is always a great place to start for seasonal observances and understanding the sacred myths. However, as we evolve our own individual Pagan practice, we should also be encouraged to develop something that reflects the land where we reside as this provides us with a deeper understanding of what the Wheel of the Year means.

Being a 'stranger in a strange land', I have long felt unconnected with the Australian landscape in which I reside, especially during summer months when all around me everything is turned to dust and my soul is yearning for something that offers the deeper and more brilliant colour of my English ancestral homeland. Through stepping beyond the confines of tradition and incorporating some of the localised aboriginal lore, not only has my appreciation of this dry barren land deepened, but so has the connection with my own ancestors and their seasonal myths.

Eclectic Paganism

By Cat Gina Cole

Eclectic Paganism is something very near and dear to me as I live it on a daily basis. I was raised with it, and it is now part of me and who I am. Eclectic Pagans are very good at borrowing and adapting that which resonates within them and using it within the constructs of their ways. Some call this magic, some call it vibrations, manifesting, or talking to the universe or deity. Being eclectic means it does not matter what you call it, as long as it works for you. To me this is the purest form of connection to deity or spirit. To be free to follow your own intuition and heart.

The beauty of Eclectic Paganism is that we decide what it means to us. We choose how to live our beliefs on a daily basis. To describe what Eclectic Paganism looks like on a daily basis would be a book by itself and it still would not cover it all. There are as many views on it as there are folks who live it.

I was raised with eclectic family cultures. My father was full blood Italian. My mother was Irish and Gypsy. I lived a life where all these cultures came together. We did a little of each. My mother and grandmother took me aside from my siblings and taught me some of the Gypsy ways that my grandmother's side of the family lived. Each day was a mix of psychism, family traditions from both sides, and magical teachings.

I was taught that all these things can live well together, and that together they build a strong foundation for living a spiritual life every day. It was easy to live this way daily with such teachers in my life. As I grew older, as is often the case, I grew away from my upbringing and got caught up in the societal world. This is easy to do as one has to work and see to the daily going on of life. I still had my base, but I was not really paying it much attention. I got swept up in what our society calls adulthood.

I was told not to tell anyone of my teachings from my mother and grandmother. This is a form of protection I am sure. Having grown up this way I naturally was a solitary practitioner. Later on I learned about Wicca, Dianic Witchcraft, and Christian Mysticism. I never did feel an affinity for any of them except the Native American ways; they resonated with me the most, but not in their entirety. Doing my own thing and holding to what was in my heart and spirit, as my grandmother taught, felt so much more right. I practiced sporadically for years, never really defining a path. I never had a feeling of knowing what I was, just that I was. It was not till later I discovered that just being is the key.

In early 2010, as my mother lay dying, my grandmother long gone, I stumbled upon my next teacher. It took some time to get me to open up and feel comfortable even talking to others about astral travel, the tarot, lucid dreaming, spirit guides, telepathy, clairvoyance and all the other things I live with on a daily basis to her, let alone in her group. I told Mom about them and she said, 'Let them in.' So I did. I very much became part of that group and now have some fabulous friends of a like mind.

In my process to rekindling all that I had been taught, I learned so much more. My psychism is a very large part of who I am and I no longer deny myself. I have come to understand that it is very important to go on a journey of self, if one is to pursue a spiritual life. Not so much self mastery, though that is important, but more self acknowledgment. A thorough knowledge of one's self and all the little stuff that makes up yourself, so you can acknowledge it and not let it interfere with the day or your efforts, to be in touch with your intuition or higher self.

Can one be Pagan and believe in energy work, higher vibrations, alternative healing, the fifth dimension, ascension, co-creation and the higher planes? My answer is, yes, as these things all come from the creative source that made us all... Pagans honour their roots and we nourish our souls, they are both parts of the whole that make us the beings we are.

This is the form my Eclectic Paganism takes, a blend of keeping an eye on my own little stuff, listening to my intuition, as I use it all the time. I attend rituals with the group for moons and holidays and when I cannot, I offer a candle to the powers that be, or just the universe, in recognition of the day. When we need rain I may be out there doing a Native American rain dance. When I do distance healing, you will hear me chanting and omming or singing the Gyatri.

I read the tarot to find things out and use various forms of divination. I use psychic techniques to effect change in myself and my world. I meditate regularly, and speak to my guides and ancestors. I enjoy the truths found in the Nine Noble Virtues of the Norse traditions. I also have regular conversations with folks about the fifth dimension and ascension and what I can do to continue raising my vibrations.

I do my best to practice these things on a regular basis while keeping an average balanced life. The key here is balance, all things in moderation. Modern Eclectic Paganism is about exploring and finding what resonates as truth to you. Check in with your intuition and higher self, be led by your spirit and heart. I tell people these days that I am a non-denominational Pagan, because I am an animist and nature based among all the other things I hold dear.

The Eclectic Pagans I hang out with and others I have experienced working with, do not believe that race, ethnic heritage, gender, or sexual orientation matter when it comes to spirituality. We try to learn from and respect other religions. Most of us see the web of energy that connects all things, the world for us is a place of infinite possibility, we have dozens of diverse traditions with somewhat differing beliefs.

We foster wisdom among our own and affirm the benefice of the universe. It is the spirit that unites us, not the details.

Lifestyle/Work/Relationships

By Irisanya

Once upon a time, there were the Reclaiming things I did and the non-Reclaiming things I did. It was so simple to keep them separate – witchy and non-witchy. But, gradually, I noticed my worlds were merging and interacting with each other. No place was this more noticeable than in my work life.

Reclaiming follows the Principles of Unity, a document that outlines everything you need to follow in order to call yourself a part of the tradition. In this document, it talks about how we use consensus to make decisions collaboratively so that all voices are heard and we can avoid power struggles. (Of course, we're not the only group to do so. Many activist groups use this tool.)

As a part of many planning cells (a.k.a. groups) within the Reclaiming tradition, I've seen consensus used, again and again. I've played the part of the facilitator and the note taker. I've been in crunchy discussions where it took a while to get to a decision.

I've practised and trained and tried and, often, succeeded within this consensus process. Alongside this work came a re-introduction to feminism (another foundation of Reclaiming) and a strong desire to build communities to support gender equality, however a person defines their gender.

But my working world doesn't always operate that way. I have some clients who are focused on the traditional looks-like-democracy-but-really-isn't model for their company. While I can still play along, the deeper my magickal practice becomes, the harder it is for me to simply allow that sort of interaction to occur.

Case in point. I was on call with a team of employees scattered across the globe. The person who was leading the call was a male-identified individual and they were talking for a while about the agenda. Another, female-identified, person on the call tried to create an agenda, and then got cut off during the conversation. The other people on the call talked over her and started talking about something else entirely.

Now, in a previous lifetime, I might have let that go and hoped things would work out (or at least I hoped others might figure something out by the time the call was supposed to be over), but not anymore.

I took a deep breath and pointed out that the woman was being interrupted and the conversation was outside the agreed upon agenda. Everyone stopped, realised what had happened, and moved back to the agreed upon conversation point.

While I'm writing this, I can see how it seems so small in relation to the various issues in the world. However, in calls that have happened since, my subtle push towards consensus process has led to more efficient calls and fewer hurt feelings.

I haven't changed the system entirely, to be sure, but without Reclaiming, I wouldn't have even had the tools to try – or to notice something was wrong.

It's not just about the tools either. I can feel the energy shifting in a conversation now, and I can tell when things aren't going the way they need to in order to support the needs of everyone in a group. I automatically speak more or less to try to support everyone's voice being heard as equally as possible.

I listen more and talk less. At the same time, when something isn't going well and someone isn't being supported, I speak up.

Certainly, I'm far from perfect, but I am blessed to have the tool of consensus. I am blessed to have seen it work – again and again – and to see how it can change the dynamics of a group.

While someone might not look at this sort of interaction as being a spell, it truly is. When you have the agreement of consensus, you have the intention for the group. When you follow the tenets of consensus, you build the container or sacred space for the discussion. You raise energy through a balanced conversation that hears all viewpoints, and you can send that energy out as you make decisions together.

Everything is magick.

Unresting Castles: Trees in Everyday Modern Paganism

By James Middleditch

The challenge is simple, yet continuously difficult – how to be truly ourselves amid the pull and tangle of our everyday lives. By 'ourselves', I mean that version of our identity that feels most authentic, when we are happiest and most content, strongest and most powerful, bold and yet serene. For Pagans, this will usually be when we have immersed ourselves in nature, perhaps as part of a ritual or to mark the turning of the Wheel of the Year, but perhaps just as part of our own need to be surrounded by it, in solitude or with our loved ones and companions. So how do we keep that feeling going when we must instead be surrounded by concrete and cars, deadlines and demands, tedium and tantrums? This is the dilemma faced by many who live and work in towns and cities, and it can cause cracks in our nature-born armour, through which disappointment and depression can seep.

I can only tell you what I strive to do, and that it helps. It's a solution that is as simple as the challenge, but one that can lead to complex and beautiful patterns of thought, which reflect the very shapes and energies of the physical stimulus – trees. This might sound obvious, but I'm not talking about the trees we travel into the country to see, those lucky, ancient souls who have been rooted far away from mankind's grid of tarmac and brick. I'm talking about the trees that have found themselves growing up amid the manmade world, and often those who have found the manmade world growing up around them. These trees are easily missed, certainly by people who have been conditioned not to see them, who instead are rushing faster than they should go to the time's-running-out-tick of the office or factory clock.

But they can be easily missed by Pagans too. These trees are undercover, waiting to assist those who know they are there.

They are as beautiful as their countryside counterparts. They even have some qualities and characteristics that make them in their own way more impressive. They are stoic amid the flow of traffic and the waft of fumes. They stand above the trudging walkers, their branches opening to the sky as far above ground level as they can reach. In winter, these trees are sculptures, patterns of paradoxically wonky symmetry; cold, bare and proud. In spring they defy the greys and blacks of the city with cheeky, childlike greens. In summer they give canopy to the concerns of the everyday world, and coolness from the friction-fuelled heat. In autumn they become what the poet Philip Larkin called 'unresting castles', bringing an organic dynamism and flow to the straight lines and corners beneath them.

I try to observe them every day, from full attention on journeys to and from work, to the corners of my eye as often as I can throughout the day. They sometimes remind me of parents in the audience as I stand on the stage of every day life and act out its expectations. They are offering secret smiles of encouragement meant only for me. They are doing what good friends always do, and reminding me who I really am.

Living Paganism

By Jay Cassels

I often wondered how our ancestors would have lived their Pagan ways back before the pact made in 3rd century Nicea. I have different imaginings of what they would make of the life Pagans have now, and I often wonder what they make of the offerings and the blessings I send to them when I honour the ancestors, not just my own linage, but all ancestors when I am working within my craft path. I have often deliberated at length with the universe about what it is to live a Pagan life in the 21st century, perhaps expecting answers within my dreams.

Through my work I have often found myself conversing, maybe even channelling a little, with one of my previous lives about what it means to be Pagan, and what it is to live a Pagan life. The answer I have found is routed in two aspects, honour and love. Honouring nature and all her beauty, being able to give back to her in small ways like healing energies, recycling, using less resources and most of all saying thank you. Above all else, saying thank you to her. After all, no one else appears to do it.

On the day of writing this essay I was reminded of the impact my ways have had on others, my partner in particular. To help paint a small picture, I do not actively discuss my ways with others; I am quite private that way, but I guess it is not what you do but how you do it. My partner, in discussion with his friend over his cat and how poorly it was, suggested offering up a prayer to Basttet, the goddess of cats. Now the prayer worked because the cat is absolutely fine, but I know there are those who would be appalled at the idea of an Egyptian goddess being associated with Pagan beliefs, but really for me why shouldn't she be? After all, god and goddess energies all come from the same source; it's only humans that differentiate to make it easier on themselves.

To me living a Pagan life is embracing all the possibilities without boundaries or barriers; to limit the potential and limit what is possible is trying to nail the wind to concrete, just to prove that it exists, to call on a god, a goddess, an angel or even a loved one is how I choose to celebrate my Pagan life. I try to send only love, compassion and unconditional understanding outwards, but I also know that it is okay to be completely human and have a dislike for someone or something.

Like my ancestors I embrace my Pagan ways and my roots. I celebrate my gods and goddesses not just at festival times but every day and in everything that I do, from working with others to writing about it. These days I don't wonder anymore, I live like they would have; freely and without limitations or boundaries, it really is the only way to be after all.

Work

By Jenny Uzzell

My relationship with Paganism has been a strange, slow affair that has always been intimately connected with my relationship with death.

I have, for as long as I can remember, had a deep, almost paralysing fear of death. Not of dying, in particular, and not (as the doctor my mother took me to suggested, after a particularly bad turn when I was 16) because I imagine myself with every imaginable disease; but a bone-deep terror of death itself. I have memories as a child of ruining family holidays by going into hysterics at seeing portraits in stately homes we visited because I could not shake the idea that the person in the picture had once been alive like me, with friends and ideas and a whole 'inner life' and that now they were dead.

My whole life, in retrospect, has been an exercise in trying to come to terms with what it means to die. It led, for example, to a brief fling with Evangelical Christianity followed by a degree in theology. I emerged from the latter with very few strong beliefs intact and over the next 20 years or so (during which time I taught religious education to 11 to 18-year-olds) I slowly became a very unwilling atheist. While I could not stand the idea that there was nothing; no God, no afterlife, no point, I could not find a way to convince my mercilessly logical and analytical mind that there was anything 'out there'.

About ten years ago, I started a master's degree at Lampeter looking at world religion. I don't think I had any particular intention to restart my old battle with death, but the Universe had other ideas!

To begin with, with the benefit of hindsight, I can see that almost everything I chose to study brought me into contact with the issue of death and the afterlife. I also met a wonderful group of people who were striving with death not only on an intellectual level, but also in terms of what could be done to improve the rather unfortunate way in which we, in this country, engage with the issue of death, dying and bereavement. Finally, I began more fully to explore my relationship with Hindu philosophy to which I had felt drawn for some time.

In particular, I felt drawn to the Hindu god of death, destruction, contradiction and regeneration, Shiva, and to the 'darkest' form of his consort, Kali. I had always been interested in this side of Hinduism intellectually, but this was far more personal and immediate. One of the attributes of Kali is that she confronts the worshipper with the stark fact of their own mortality and invites them to come to terms with it. I began to read all I could and even to dream about Shiva. I built altars in my home and finally felt that I had a spirituality that took my fears seriously rather than dismissing them or trying to shoo them away with superficial comforts that made no sense. I had had a long relationship with Paganism by this time and while I felt drawn to it I never quite felt that it was where I fitted. The realisation that the ideas I had drawn from Hinduism fitted well into the huge 'idea-scape' that is Paganism was a massive revelation and a release. I finally felt that I could call myself Pagan.

Another thing that happened around this time was that I got divorced, quite amiably, from my husband. Not long after he left, I was able to go on holiday to Greece with a close friend and we visited the site of the Eleusinian Mysteries, about 14km from Athens. This was a dream come true for me as I had always been fascinated by Ancient Greek religion and I had completed a piece of work on mystery religions as part of my studies. As we were finishing our tour, I found myself alone by the tiny temple to Hades next to the cave, where the very earliest rites at this site were carried out, and which was believed at the time to be an entrance to Hades' realm. I had a strong sense of the presence of Death as a gentle and benevolent companion who had always been with me. It felt like making up with an old enemy, a strong sense that all was well, and that Death and I were to have a close relationship. While I was profoundly moved by this, I could not easily have explained what had happened; I had seen and heard nothing.

Shortly after this I met my present partner, who had been a funeral director for many years. He worked for a large company and was increasingly dissatisfied with the impersonal way that people were treated. Three years ago we had the opportunity to set up our own funeral home and so to my astonishment I now find myself caring for the dead and the bereaved on a daily basis. I finally feel as if I am doing what I was always meant to do. Our vision is to enable people to play a much bigger role in the care of their dead and in the rituals that surround death. We aim to act as a resource and a source of information and to help people to find new ways of doing what they really want to do when the time comes to let someone go. I have also just started my doctorate, exploring the ways in which Pagans, among others, are innovating new funeral rituals that speak to us in the present. I have still not fully come to terms with death, I am not sure it is possible, for me, at least; but I finally feel as if I am using my life in a way that can be genuinely helpful to others. In a way, I feel as if I have found the vocation that my whole life has been a preparation for.

Druidry, Glastonbury, UK

By John Awen

My name is John Awen. I live in Glastonbury with my wife and our pets. I have been treading this path for about five years now and thoroughly enjoy giving myself to this earth-based tradition.

For me personally, Druidry is a state of heart. I am a Druid all the time, the same as it is within me all the time, not just when I put on robes, in fact I hardly ever wear robes, unless I am performing a ceremony. For me, it's the inner connection that shines, lights the way and reveals the path we find ourselves on, that's what really matters.

For two years, my wife and I lived 'off grid' so to speak. We lived in a log cabin, with no mains fed gas or electricity. This was a tough time, but within that, it was also a very special and magical time. We looked after quite a variety of animals, including sheep, pigs, turkeys, ducks, chickens and even peacocks.

Living so sparsely and in such close proximity to the land, five acres to be exact, which we rented, obviously we were going to connect very deeply with it and all the nature around.

I was following a Druid path before we lived this way, but living as we did for two years, installed within and upon me many traits, empathy, compassion, love and honour for all creation and a deeper understanding of myself and people as a whole.

I certainly got a very good understanding of the universal Karmic law as well while living as we did. The spider's web, that connects us all intrinsically, is unseen, often unfelt and disregarded. Once you live simply, with no clutter of the modern world around you, no lighting, no TV, just two of you and a whole load of animals, you are either going to go insane, or embrace it and totally work with it all, we chose the latter.

To have had this chance was incredible, to see new life being born up front and too often assist with it, was so beautiful. On the other hand, I have also been with many animals while they have passed away, to calm them hopefully and not leave them on their own.

I totally believe that to have connected so deeply and tightly with the trees, animals and the land, and to have embraced all the elements, as we had to, helped me personally to evolve, physically, mentally and spiritually. To have shared birthing and passing with such a wide range of animals was truly humbling, very emotional and many tears were shed, but to actually be a part of it has and will always stand me in good stead as I follow my Druid path; just now with a deeper rooted connection to life, death and all that is sacred in this world.

We had no mains electricity when we lived in the log cabin. We had one solar panel that charged up a 12v battery. That was the only power we had constantly and we had to go easy with that, especially during the winter months when rays from the sun are not always very strong. We had a strip of LEDs, which were sufficient to read and write by and for my partner to spin fleeces and knit. The strange thing is, now we live in a flat with all mod cons, if we get up in the night, we still don't turn the lights on. We just don't think about it now, which is good for us, as it keeps our minds sharper and is obviously better for the environment in which we now live. It's so easy, for any of us, to take for granted the use of mains electricity, gas and other utilities. It only seems that when you have actually lived without these things that you realise they are not really a necessity, just a convenience of the world and society in which we live. This abuse of mod cons and blatant waste of resources is undoubtedly having a massive knock-on effect on us, our children and this beautiful planet, which we are only guardians/caretakers of for the short time we are here. We really must start to think about what our actions are doing, simply before it's too late

To have lived as we did remote and cut off to some extent, I know has helped instil deep within me just how precious this planet and all contained within it really is. Even though I walked a Druid path before, I was nowhere near as connected to the elements, to animals, trees, myself and others; how could I have been? It is from living this way each and every day, seeing flooding of biblical proportions, hurricane winds and only being in a cabin, that really connected me to just how ferocious and totally unpredictable the weather can be. There were times when we were both frightened, helpless and scared, but we survived and that has left its mark within and without my wife and myself. It was a very humbling way to live and exist. It brought us closer together and within that it helped us to become who we are today, to honour all creation, to work with, not against, the weather and seasons, to see the natural beauty that is everywhere in abundance, to appreciate the start of a new day and the end of the day, to actually watch the sunrise and the sunsets, to feel the temperature change so closely. It was certainly an eye opener and a way of life that I know will stand me in good stead for the rest of my life and while treading my Druid path.

New Year 2010

By Lady Laeynarrie Auvresti

The tail end of 2009 was the catalyst that began a whole new life. I found myself alone with three young children, one of which was a newborn as of late November. The living arrangement was faulty at best, a death trap at worst. I was defeated and depressed, knowing I was not in a healthy situation.

By that time, I had already been in regular contact with a small group of people I had met online. They were there each night as I dealt with being abandoned by the baby's father and the stress of being bed-bound through pregnancy complications. I found this group while searching for 'witchy' companions in my first real experience with online communication. Miraculously, I am blessed to still be in contact with some of them. Each day during this time, they helped keep me focused on who I wanted to be – who I knew I had always been. Unfortunately, I'd always had to hide this aspect of myself from almost everyone I knew.

Then one day, shortly before New Year's Eve, I had an angry moment of clarity. Two things came to mind. First, I remembered that a friend I made within that past year recognised and accepted exactly who I am, which made me realise that I am not crazy. The second thought was, 'I am alone.' With no one really around regularly anymore, I could finally tear down the façade. I could dance around my room again (to the delight of my children); I could pull out my long hidden books and start studying and pouring back into my passion.

With a new goal in mind, I consulted with my online friends and involved one physical friend (I remember wishing I could contact that friend I mentioned earlier). We planned out a burning ceremony to be performed on New Year's Eve. I thought long and hard about the intentions of the burning: what exactly did I want? I carefully wrote it all out and on December 31, 2009, into midnight, we clumsily performed the ceremony. I remember watching my folded up piece of paper sear and scorch and feeling a very noticeable stirring within. I knew something must be working.

The following weeks became a blur of adjustment mixed with trial and error. It seemed my desire to unblock my gifts and senses was well heard. For about a month, my home was the place to be to experience the paranormal. It wasn't until the sudden reappearance of that inspiring friend that the chaos began to get sorted out. He helped me focus and encouraged my abilities. He taught me a few tricks and helped me wrestle the demons. On one particularly emotional night, he made me promise not to give up on love. Ever since then, he has been my best friend, my partner in crime, and now my husband.

I frequently reminisce about that crucial time period; about all the changes, growth, and loss that exploded after that fateful New Year's burning. For quite some time, it was a whirlwind of fear, excitement, learning, and awakening. There was the harsh heartbreak of being disowned by the family I grew up with on the grounds of religious differences. I realised then that it was a situation of completely rebuilding my life – rebuilding myself – from the ground up.

I use that memory, that defining moment of my life, to reflect back and remind myself how much I've grown. For me, it is a personal testimony of growth, inner strength, and the power of self-dedication. I am nowhere near the end of my journey, but, for this life, there is no final exam. Mistakes are allowed. Pauses and breaks are alright. Moments of doubt and fear are expected. There is no real 'right way' except within your own definitions and goals.

I've learned more about myself since that burning than I ever dreamed of figuring out beforehand. Initially, I thought I was incapable of surviving alone; that I was weak and worthless. My childhood was corrupted way too early and it took its toll. I won't go into the sob story, but I'm sure some of you can relate. Now, however, with the new-found determination to do right by myself and the need to encourage my children to remain true to themselves, I've learned how strong I really am. I've seen how the support of positive and loving people and my own blossoming goals have transformed my life.

Let us fast forward to 2014. Not only have I grown personally into a strong individual, mother, wife, and sister, I have also achieved the beginnings of my goals. Through innumerable hours of study and practise, I have become the equivalent of a High Priestess (I have technically been awarded the title through a training coven, but I tested out of the programme rather than taking the full training). I have even begun writing my own lessons, both as a way to make sure I know it and as my way of helping others who want to learn.

These days, aside from focusing on the beautiful family I have grown with, I spend my energy on helping those who call on me and spreading as much positive energy as I can. I co-manage an amazing online group that I created a few years ago that, as of this essay, is just shy of 100 members. I write as much as I can, meditate as often as possible, play with my crystals and herbs, light a candle every full moon, and plan our dream of a spiritual centre. Most importantly, though, I prove to my children and to those who thought I was nothing that you can do anything you put your mind to; that magick and miracles are everywhere, and that you (yes YOU) are stronger than you think you are.

Lifestyle

By Lyn Thurman

I am very much a woman of my time. I have a husband, children, my own business, a semi-detached house with the obligatory mortgage and a family car parked on the driveway. To the casual observer, I'm just a mid-life mum with nothing particularly special or different about me. Nothing at all that screams 'witch'. But the more observant passer-by might just notice the broomstick-riding voodoo doll dangling from my car rear-view mirror. The clues are there if you look for them.

Witch is still a loaded label to pin proudly to your lapel. Everyone seems to have a different opinion of what makes a witch, and what he or she does. It has become erroneously synonymous with Wiccan, but I prefer my spirituality pre-Gardnerian revolution. I'm a seeker of the old way, always looking for the spirit in my bones.

I would love to tell you that my experiences of being a 21st century witch are full of saucy antics and scandalous going-ons but, alas, that's just Hollywood (and maybe a little wishful thinking on my part). Life is remarkably normal.

There are subtle differences that set me apart from the non-Pagan community. For me, it comes down to values and beliefs, not where I do my grocery shopping. My life is very spirit driven; I follow signs, I look for omens, I find inspiration in the whispers of the wind. When I need guidance, my first port of call is a tarot deck rather than a therapist. Everything has meaning and significance. A coincidence is never merely a coincidence.

My husband and I share similar beliefs, which makes raising our daughter simpler. We homeschool her, something not widely practiced in the UK, and we encourage her to think about her spirituality in a way she wouldn't be taught in the school system.

Of course, she's young and our beliefs have influenced hers, but she's free to change, evolve or adopt beliefs. I wouldn't have it any other way, but at the moment she's content to be a witchling. We stare at the moon together, she delights in books about ancient Egypt, and she worries over the spirits of animals.

Respect of Mother Nature, and understanding her wisdom, is a big part of my life. I'm a vegetarian because I couldn't ethically be part of the way meat products are sourced. Life, in all forms, is sacred. I believe we have everything we need to heal and thrive on our beautiful planet — my cupboards are full of herbs and spices, not just for healing, but also to harness the power of the plant in magic. I spend happy hours in the kitchen making potions, lotions, oils, and washes.

Whereas, it seems, most families in the UK head out to a theme park for fun and thrills, you will find me away from the crowds. The ancient pathways, standing stones, burial mounds, ruins, and places mentioned in folklore books are where I feel called to visit. I have a belief, and it's been with me forever, that answers are in the past but there are clues in the present. My choice of books and, as a writer my choice of writing, reflects this. I have a limited scope of interests with spirituality at the core.

I identify as a witch, a wise woman, because I don't know what other label fits me. My spiritual practices are simple. I find my temple in nature, particularly by the sea. At home, my rituals usually just involve candles and oil; I'm not a fan of long ceremony. I remember the ancestors, particularly my maternal mothers who have passed from this life but from whom life is given to me.

I'm a modern Pagan woman, following the spirit in my bones, and always seeking the old ways to make sense of the world I live in today.

Respect

By Mabh Savage

'So how come you were off work? Busy polishing your goat's skull?'

The other lad with him laughs, and I feel my face grow red with anger and embarrassment; embarrassment that I have no words to express how deeply this offends and upsets me; embarrassment that the people laughing and making these comments are not strangers, not enemies, not even ignorant acquaintances.

These are my friends.

Shocking, yes? How can good friends, good *people,* take my beliefs and twist them so? Use them for fun?

Because as a Pagan, I keep things close to my chest. I don't wear a badge saying, *'I'm a Pagan. Ask me how!'* I don't broadcast my spirituality to all and sundry because, quite frankly, it's none of anyone else's business how I live my life and what spirits or deities I choose to speak to.

But of course, I took the drastic step of writing about my experiences, for those that are interested and may wish to walk a nature-based path themselves. This means that my good, *non-Pagan* friends, who will *never* read my books, are suddenly interested in the fact that I am a self-confessed Pagan.

It never even occurred to me that there were 'negative' (and I use this word grudgingly) connotations to being a Pagan.

'So, do you all go to orgies?'

'You dance around naked at the full moon, right?'

'Oh Mabh won't be in work tomorrow, she'll be out howling at the moon somewhere.'

And I'm not the only one who experiences this. One of my good friends, a fantastic priestess and coven maid, was harangued at work by a born again Christian who tried to tell her she was in league with the devil. I mean, for goodness sake...

Who has the time and energy to waste on that kind of thinking?

So now everyone knows I am a Pagan and 90 per cent of those people think it's weird. The truth is, *I* think it's weird to follow one god (of any denomination) and the teachings of one book (of any culture). I think it's weird to be completely atheist; to decide that there is nothing in this universe beyond ourselves. I think it's weird not to see the magic in the turn of the seasons, or the changing of the moon, or the ebb and swell of the tides. I think it's weird not to smell spring on a February afternoon, or the returning snow on a March morning. Most of all, I know I am blessed and gifted to be able to experience those things for myself.

But you don't hear me calling any of these people weirdoes, right? I didn't ask if any of them were off work because they were at home polishing their Virgin Mary statue!

That's called respect, peoples. Respect, kindness and understanding. We all have a path to walk; it isn't right to trample on anyone else's and muddy the way for them.

So I smile at the comments and am tolerant of the ignorance, and as much as I can I try to educate and inform rather than being angry or self-righteous. People ask me what being a Pagan means; the cute answer is 'read my book', but I tend to lead with the answer, *'It's about understanding your place in the world; understanding that everything is connected, everything changes, and every change causes something else to change. You are just one piece in that transformation, and when you feel that connection to everything around you, you can truly begin to understand yourself.'*

It must be working. At Christmas last year, one of the guys at work who had mocked previously went out of his way to get me a Yule card instead of the Christmas cards he gave everyone else. I grinned as I opened it. See: even the smallest change is magic.

My Personal Pagan Beliefs

By Marie Strang

I consider myself an agnostic and a Pagan, which means that I hold that Nature is sacred, but I don't believe any deities actually exist. However, I find the idea of deities valuable as archetypes and as mythology. Some might say I am a Humanistic Pagan, and that's fine, too. To me, all deities are imaginary and to worship any deity as sacred takes the emphasis off what is truly sacred, i.e. Nature.

The ancient Greeks mentioned Logos and Mythos. I see us as having a logical side (Logos) and a non-literal side that craves stories and dreams and mythology (Mythos). So although I don't believe in deities literally, I find that personifying concepts as deities appeals to the Mythos side of me that wants stories and anything imaginative and intuitive. Deities as archetypes can be inspiring. In that way, deities have their uses even if they aren't real. I think the harm is done when people make deities more important than reality. Susan B Anthony said it best: 'I distrust those people who know so well what God wants them to do because I notice it always coincides with their own desires.'

I try to live in the moment, not the past or too far into a future that only may be. I believe we have some sort of soul and I believe in reincarnation. These beliefs come from my own personal experiences. I base my spirituality on my experiences and not on someone else's book or faith. Although I believe in reincarnation, I don't think it does much good to focus too much on past or future lives. No matter how many lives I've had or will have, I will never have this exact life or body or set of experiences ever again and that makes this life as special and sacred as any other and it should be valued as much as any other.

I don't see a conflict between science and Nature. Science

seeks to explain the natural world. Knowing how complex the universe is and how it all evolved so slowly over billions of years just reinforces my Pagan beliefs that Nature itself is sacred.

Since we are part of Nature, that makes us sacred, too. Some people who believe in deities tend to devalue anything or anyone they don't think is sanctified by their deity. I have found this attitude to be most prevalent in monotheistic religions, but even some of the Pagan religions sometimes put more emphasis on deity instead of Nature. How differently would we treat each other if we kept in mind that Nature is sacred and so are we and that no one group of people is the favourite of a deity, but we are all equal because we are all sacred?

Although I don't believe in God or in gods, the idea of a Goddess or goddesses appeals to me. To paraphrase Mary Daly: 'As long as God is male, the male will be God.' I think women need the archetype of the Goddess as a role model and as a method of empowerment. I could never abide the sexism in mainstream religions. The equality of men and women in most Pagan religions always appealed to me. Equality of the sexes (and genders) and of all people is important to me.

Sometimes I participate in religious rituals, either as a solitary or with a group, and while I enjoy these rituals, I don't find them necessary in order to be spiritual. Rituals can offer insight sometimes and they certainly appeal to the part of ourselves that needs Mythos, but I feel most spiritual just sitting quietly in the woods. Even ordinary, everyday life can be spiritual when you take time to reflect on the fact that we exist and are alive and all those little atomic particles make up every one and every thing in infinite variety throughout this universe and possibly other universes.

These beliefs and philosophies influence my daily life. I try to buy products that were made without cruelty to people or animals or to the environment. Whenever possible I try to eat food that is organically and sustainably grown and that is fair trade. I was appalled to find out that slave labour is used to produce chocolate in some parts of the world, so I look for chocolate made by companies that have assurances on their labels that they don't use slave labour or otherwise engage in harmful practices.

It isn't always easy to find products made by fair practices, and such products are usually more expensive. I make my own things when possible, if I have the skill or the time. The best case scenario might be to live in a cabin out in the woods and be completely self-reliant, but that isn't practical and I don't think it would make a big difference in the long run. Besides, that would be running away. I try to make a difference however I can, where I am.

Nature is sacred and everything in Nature is sacred and should be respected, therefore I strive to do my best in my own way to improve the world, and to be kind, and as the Wiccans say, do no harm.

The Teachings of Children

By Romany Rivers

My son was just two. He stood forlornly at the kitchen window, hand pressed against the glass and visibly upset. When I asked him what was wrong he turned towards me, a leaf held in his little fingers, offering it to me. 'Fix the tree,' he asked me. 'The leaf, it fell over. Fix the tree?'

I knelt beside him as he pointed to the tree outside the window and took the leaf from his insistent hands. I saw the first touches of autumn around us, trees kissed with different colours, the wind tugging a few leaves loose to scatter across the grass. As gently as I could, I looked into his tear-filled brown eyes and told him that I could not fix the tree. I explained that when a leaf fell down, it could not be stuck back on, that some things could not be undone.

'The tree is broken!' he cried.

'No, no,' I replied.

As best I could I explained that it was normal, that autumn was just a part of the cycle and come spring the tree would grow new green leaves. I do not think he believed my heartfelt explanation. I can only hope he trusted me in his moment of uncertainty.

We learned so much from that moment. He learned that Mama could not fix everything; that some things were beyond even my reach. At such a young age he learned that not every hurt could be kissed away, not everything broken could be fixed, and that the world around him could change quickly. I learned the power of compassion even in the absence of understanding. I learned to see the world through my son's eyes. I learned to see the cycles and seasons of the year in a new perspective, in a way that my adult mind had long overlooked by taking these patterns of nature for granted. My son had to hope that the leaves would be restored; I just assumed they would as they do every year. I learned that I had become blind to the beauty and wonder of the world around me; that at some point I had continued to look but not truly see. My two-year-old tearful child taught me to reconnect with nature through the eyes of first discovery.

When people learn that I am Pagan and that I have two children it is not uncommon to be asked how my spirituality affects my parenting. Yet I have often found it to be the other way around. Parenting, from as early as dreaming of a family, affects my spirituality. As much as my beliefs help to form my opinions around the raising of children, it is the raising of children that deepens my beliefs. I learn so much about myself from parenting. I discover all my weak spots, my hot button issues, how far my patience extends, how grumpy I really am in the morning. I also discover my strengths, how calm I can be in a crisis, how quickly I can resolve a conflict, how creative and inspiring I can be. I have learned about qualities I never knew I possessed, and I have learned about parts of myself that I want to change. I realised how one small person's emotional state can impact an entire environment. I have learned more about Reiki from working with my children during times of pain and stress, peace and snuggles. I have discovered new reasons to meditate. I have reconnected with the power of imagination. I have explored new creative expressions. I have created homes for faeries and chased an invisible cat that my son plays with. I have hugged trees and patted rocks and smiled when my children declared that the trees 'felt better'. I have learned the power of standing by core principles and beliefs in the face of adversity. I discovered that pregnancy, childbirth and breastfeeding can be simultaneously wonderful and awful, that personal power is important, that community support is invaluable, that our spiritual, mental, emotional and physical health are interconnected, and that this whole process can be seen as a hero's journey. I learned the power of energy exchange through skin contact.

I connected deeply with the Feminine Divine in ways I had never experienced before. I have learned to find joy and beauty in simple pleasures. I observe nature, the seasons and the cycles of the year in a whole new way. I understand love and grief, laughter and anxiety, planting and harvesting better than ever before. Within the trials and tribulations of raising toddlers who swing from one emotion to the next, I learned to find – or at least to always strive for – personal balance. I work with the elements more consciously and more frequently now.

My kitchen has become my most practical magical space, and my home office has become my spiritual sanctuary. My garden has become a world of wonder, and our daily walks have become ways to express our interconnectedness of all things. Bedtime stories have become wisdom teachings, and moments of peace and quiet take on more importance for my overall health and well-being. In facing my future with children, I have also learned to heal my past.

So I find myself hesitating, blinking and bemused when faced with the question, 'Do you raise your children as Pagan?' No, I think to myself. No I don't. I believe that my children are Pagan, and it is they who raise me.

Mother Goddess

By Rosie Weaver

The Sacred Mother Goddess is an integral part of my life, she always has been. She influences my politics, my thoughts, my acts and my deeds.

When I was a little girl, back in my school days in the 1960s, I recall always having many questions regarding religions. Christianity was spoon fed to us daily, we had to sit cross-legged every morning in assembly, listening to Bible quotes from Bible bashers, as they were called, the wrath of God became instilled into us on a regular basis.

Frequently I tried asking questions I considered to be valid, questions such as: where was God's wife? How was it possible for a male God to give birth? Why was Eve so evil for eating an apple?

My questions were always met with similar responses. 'Yours is not to question my girl.' 'That's just the way it is.' 'Because it is God's law and rule and he decreed it.'

All of this seemed nonsensical to me, the God philosophy just didn't hold water to a young girl with an overly curious mind.

As I grew older I began to notice the huge imbalance in religions where women were practically excluded from just about every male-dominated monotheistic belief system. As I researched more in my teenage years I grew to understand that the entire Patriarchal system had been set up by men, for men. All to divide and conquer half of the human race (my half – female).

Looking at the comparative religions led me to research Paganism and women's deeper mysteries. In my new understanding I realised that the original Earth religion had in fact been Goddess oriented.

The Divine Feminine had been recognised from the dawn of

time as sacred both within women and Mother Earth. She had been honoured up until a point whereby Patriarchy usurped Her, purely for exploitative reasons.

A few greedy, selfish men used religions and politics (which went hand in hand) to suppress every aspect of the Goddess in Her full glory. This process resulted in all things associated with the Goddess throughout the world being stamped out and driven underground. Women were hounded and put to death as witches, as were some supportive men too.

No one dared to question this brutal system for fear of the consequences. The exploitative process followed through every aspect of existence. The medical establishment as we now know it took over from the natural remedies and village midwives, all gaining a bad reputation through the authority of Patriarchy. Anything that did not conform to this system gained a dark and sinister reputation.

Stories of devil worship and witchcraft were perpetuated by the Church. Every country village was overseen by a pastoral shepherd ensuring his flock followed suit. Those who refused, for whatever reason, were seen as outcasts and shunned by other villagers amidst a flurry of suspicion.

The old Pagan sacred sites where a tutelary Goddess would have been honoured and celebrated on a seasonal basis became quickly dismantled. Churches were often built over these sites. Many of Britain's most famous churches and cathedrals were originally Goddess sites. For example, there are legends that St Paul's Cathedral, in London, had once been a Roman shrine to the Goddess Diana, and evidence of a temple to the Goddess Isis has also been discovered in London.

The deeper I went down the rabbit hole the more it became apparent with my own personal research, this further led me to feel a huge sense of injustice for all that had been done in the name of male-dominated religions.

I learned that we live on a planet that is infiltrated by greed and exploitation. I learned about the way the planet, which at one time had been considered a Sacred Mother, is totally used and abused for man's selfish gain.

The fracking issues we now face, along with genetically modified organisms (GMOs), can be related to the same principles as the treatment of all that is feminine throughout the world.

Everything we once considered hallowed has been corrupted and is now seen as something to simply be used for personal gain. The dots can be joined, and sadly they do.

Male privilege and entitlement have become the norm; one where not all men partake, but very few speak out. We live in a global rape culture, which has become normalised. Listen to the words of a lot of the rap music, watch the videos. Even many of the children's video games are horribly brutal and violent towards women. And this we generally accept as normal society.

I cannot comprehend that in this century, with all the wondrous advancements that have been made, so little has been done to address the human condition.

We have been relegated to second class citizens from a time that once honoured and celebrated our divine essence.

All of this awareness has greatly influenced my life. I'm now a grandmother of seven. I do not want my granddaughters growing up into this same world of imbalance that I have lived through; where one in three women will experience some form of male-dominated violence/sexual abuse in their lifetime; as myself and daughters, friends and women I have known have.

I don't want my grandsons growing up to believe this is the right way forward; that male entitlement is all that matters.

We all matter, in fact the word for 'mother' actually derives from the word 'matter'. This includes all of Nature i.e. the Divine Feminine inherent in all life. Not something to be used, abused and exploited.

I do whatever I can to generate this awareness on a day-to-day basis. I protest as many humanitarian and planetary issues as possible and speak out about a return to the source, who I know as Isis of 10,000 names. As Her Priestess, I am also Her daughter returned.

Some people listen, occasionally I sense that it does make a difference. Some don't, and continue to shop the pain away.

In 100 years from now I hope those that may be reading this, are living in full realisation and that balance has been fully restored for the whole of humanity and our beautiful planet.

Please Goddess, let it be so...

Political Pagan

By Talis Kimberley-Fairbourn

I always say that if you ask 12 assorted Pagans what defines their faith, you'll get 13 different answers, because one of them will have changed their mind by the time you finish.

I think that's largely true, but one of the three defining principles for me as a 20-year patchwork Pagan, and latterly with very Druidic leanings, is a reverence and respect for the natural world we inhabit. I think that's something the vast majority of Pagans of any flavour would share.

My journey into politics has been powered by two things. The first is my refusal to accept the raging inequality that is currently increasing in our society, leaving many without means, dignity or hope. The second is my lifelong awareness that our small blue planet is finite in its ability to absorb what we do to it, without damaging the very systems on which we depend for food, water, and air. That some people seem able to pretend otherwise continues to astonish me. That they are very often the people in power who make decisions affecting the seizure and disposal of resources, the way energy is gathered and utilised by society, and the degree to which the delicate web of interacting lives and systems is brutalised for profit, convinced me that the time was past for trying to change their minds. They know, and they have chosen not to care.

To me, therefore, it became plain that to protect what I held dear in the living world around me, I had to do what I could not to change the minds of those in power, but to change those in power – for better people. The deeply flawed political system we have is nonetheless the only alternative to blood in the streets – so I put my shoulder to the wheel, and started to act where I had watched, to join what I had critiqued, and to stand where I had commented on the empty space.

Specifically, I saw that we have come to feel both disempowered, and very unrepresented by our elected 'representatives'. They are, so often, not the best of us, but the one who most wanted the job, and those positions are increasingly the gift of a small group of existing powerful people. This is not what democracy looks like.

It's hard enough to get local people to stand as Parish Councillor, from fear, from lack of confidence, from a mistaken belief that someone else will do a better job. There's also apathy, and a sense of not having the time or the knowledge to do it well. How much more do most of the people we meet on a day-to-day basis feel completely unable to contemplate standing for higher office? The decision to stand in a General Election crept up on me, and I found I had made it without having to think about making it. It was a done deal. I wanted to make my stand against those who think that fracking is a good idea, against those who think that an ocean full of plastic is not a problem, and that documented changes in our climate are a reasonable price for economic gain. Such people act with stunning indifference to the wellbeing of the people they are supposed to represent and the rest of the natural world besides.

This is not a path a Druid could choose for fun or profit, but a task that requires all one's will and energy, in the defence of what cannot defend itself, in stewardship of the land that sustains us all.

I Can't Wait

By Rufus Brock Maychild

For a Pagan Planet, that is. I'm not impatient by nature, just getting old, whiskers all a-whitened, and entitled to a free bus pass. I just don't have that long! I've been Pagan, and 'active with it' almost all of my adult life – for 40 years by now. In that time Neo-Paganism has grown greatly in numbers, has achieved public visibility and been acceptance by the state, but a Pagan Planet doesn't seem much closer. When I began, when Goddess first called to me, the idea of a Pagan Planet wasn't on the agenda at all – at least not among Neo-Pagans, though I'm sure the many millions across the globe still dedicated to their Ancestral Pagan traditions had different perspectives. Back then, Neo-Paganism was buried in 'the occult' and operated as an initiatory secret society.

In 1980, at the last gasp of the Cold War, I founded a group named Pagans Against Nukes (PAN). Our mission statement, on the banner of our magazine The Pipes of PAN, included 'The re-establishment of a culture that lives in harmony with Mother Earth'. We were very busy for a number of years. PAN hosted the first open Pagan ritual at the Glastonbury Green Gathering in 1982, again in 1983 and held the first Pagan camp of our own in 1984. Fundamental to our process was to establish a definition of 'Pagan' as including all those for whom Mother Earth was at the centre of their spirituality.

We called directly on Pan and on Gaia to crack the concrete of the nuclear bunkers. We marched and demonstrated and camped. Some of our hands embraced the bases with tens of thousands of others. We called on the Wild Hunt to haunt the bombers (and transform their consciousness). Years later, the bombs have indeed gone from Greenham Common – the nightingale and the Dartford warbler sing there again. But away from there the world seems in a very dangerous state, awash in blood and militarism (a chunk paid for by my unwilling taxes). The new millennium has brought not enlightenment but rather a horror of new atrocities. We face the clear possibility of an unprecedented ecocide, not even just human extinction and a world bequeathed to cockroaches, but conceivably the death of Gaia Herself. Just to cope with daily life we are in denial of most of this. But the pain and the despair that this brings to us means that we still have connection to Gaia, to our fellow humans, and to all our relations here upon Her.

So what is to be done? Paganism has often (usually as an insult) been termed a 'fertility religion'. At this time, perhaps the kindest magic we could ask of Gaia would be a sterility plague. There are just too many humans here – and I write this only too aware that my own attempts at living lightly still leave my footprint on at least a couple of planets. Many New Age writers have spoken of planetary change and less folks being here in future – but most of the conceivable ways this might happen involve the survivors in a lot of gravedigging, as well as the first victims being those least deserving of such. Direct divine intervention would certainly be appreciated, but I don't think I should hold my breath waiting for it. Even less would I hold my breath for science and rationalism to fix things. Our own activism is vital, both physical and magical, but take care – a burnt-out firework isn't much use for the future.

I feel both a bit sad and a bit annoyed that in this life I'm not likely to see that Pagan Planet. I'm quite happy with the concept of reincarnation – without it everything seems literally without meaning anyway. But I've just become a grandparent for the first time. From the viewpoint of eternity, perhaps the survival of my genes doesn't much matter, but my hormones tell me otherwise. I fear for the future of this innocent infant, as for all the others. I hope indeed he is one of the wise of old returned to us, for the world surely needs them. And for myself, I would like there to be someone around in the future to call me back with love.

I have always believed that our Paganism can and should be at the heart of the Great Turning. For me, the Spirit of Gaia is real, not just some metaphor. We will not Turn if we deny Her. It is easy to assume that we are the good guys, recycling our bottles, paper, food waste and so on, and invoking 'peace and love'. I think we also need to examine ourselves and our spiritual practices. As a part of that I suggest time is due to make a change to that most basic feature of Paganism – the Circle. For a long time, most people have made the Circle a barrier to the world by striding its boundary. They have made a hiding place and an enclosure of the magic. It's time instead for our Circles to be open, every one of them an active conduit through which the Spirits of the Land, the Ancestors and the Shining Ones, our Goddesses and Gods, may reclaim the Earth.

So I ask you to give up on your perambulations (with or without the threatening blades and the imagined barriers of blue fire). Instead, Call your Circles into being from the Centre, the Source of All that connects you to the Cosmos. Visualise instead the Waters of the Deep rising forth in purification of your sacred space as the Fountain of Life. Greet the Unquenchable Fires of Heaven as the consecration of your sacred space, rising like a new volcano. Ask the Four Winds to blow their blessings to and through you. Join your hands in trust and join your Circle to the greater Circle of Being.

So May the Web of Life be Renewed.

Merry Meet Again!

What is that Hellenic Witch up to Now?

By Samantha Leaver

A typical day for the Hellenic witch starts like any other witch starts their day.

Set the cauldron simmering.

Take the rats' tails out the freezer for later.

Summon the spirit of the broom to sweep.

Or perhaps not!

It's more like peeling my face off the pillow, have a wash, get dressed, and head downstairs. Pretty average I'd say until…

I wish my Agathos Daimon, the protective snake-shaped spirit of my home that brings good luck and prosperity to the household, a blessed day ahead, say a morning devotional to a deity of the day e.g. Friday = Aphrodite, remove last night's meal offering from Hestia's sacred kitchen altar, and switch on the battery-operated candle that represents her fiery hearth. This is a Saturday, if it were a working day I'd be running out the door because I'm late.

It's the darkest phase of the moon, the day before the New Moon, or Noumenia. At sundown because just to be awkward Hellenic worship is based on a lunar calendar that starts at the New Moon it's Hekate's Depinon. Depinon simply means main meal, and the dark phase is dedicated to Hekate, 'the bringer of the light'. This meal can happen any time before the first sliver of moon appears in the sky and for me consists of anything that includes garlic, onions, eggs, honey and wine for libation; culinary delights sacred to Hekate.

It's a time of purification, clean like a banshee day – mind, body, spirit, and space. I take stock of the month's ups and downs, tie up loose ends, and prepare to welcome the new lunar phase; this practice seems to be fairly universal in the witchy world.

There's also scholarly thought that this day is important to the less fortunate. The ancients would leave an offering to the Goddess outside (preferably at the crossroads). If it's not too cold/wet I'll nip out with any leftovers from the meal, otherwise these sacred offerings get wrapped up in kitchen towel so they don't touch other rubbish and are popped into the bin. Anyway, I digress, the poor would eat these offerings. Therefore some say this is a good day to donate food, money or time to the homeless or charity; this also boosts favour with the Gods for the Hellenic witch always practices sex safe! Ha! Sorry…moderation (not too much now ya hear?), reciprocity (you rub my back, I'll rub yours) and hospitality (hello, come on in) to name but a few of the ethical ideals that go along with 'harm none but take no rubbish'.

The evening itself is of quiet contemplation, I will feast, journal, burn incense and feel a bubble of excitement build for the celebrations to come…for this is one of three celebratory evenings to welcome in the new month and moon phase for the Hellenic witch next door. Tomorrow will see a change of gear and pace as the month begins anew, once again.

Being a Pagan

By Scott Irvine

I see our planet the Earth as a living organism known as the Great Mother, or Gaia, on which humanity journeys through space and time in a great cycle of possibilities and opportunities. It is an experience open to anyone who is aware of the ride. Existing on our planet are myriad spirit forces that coexist with us. Everything is infused with its own energy; every river, well and spring, every tree, bush and plant is awash with spirit life. Nature is the connection between Heaven and Earth, between the spirit world of our subconscious and the world of matter that is our conscious world. Even inanimate objects, such as rock, metal and plastic, or even vehicles for that matter, have at their core a spirit that allows the object to connect to everything else in the universe, including us. Being a Pagan in today's world of capitalism and quantum physics is as important to us now as it was to the ancients. We humans have lost the ability to experience our true potential within the universe. We need the Gods and Goddesses of the past to protect us from today's Gods of Power, Money, Fame and Celebrity, to help awaken us from sleepwalking to oblivion. The God and Goddess energy is in everything and is everywhere.

Ever since I was legal to ride a motorbike, my lifestyle has been that of a biker. I love the freedom (sometimes) of the open road and the thrill of slicing my way through the elements, feeling the air blast over my body, smelling the countryside aromas and listening to nature competing with the whine of the engine. The spirit of man and machine are connected with the spirit of existence becoming one with the universe. I have always felt the presence of a higher force riding with me, mixing its energy with mine, the motorbike and the universe, protecting me against the dangers of the road. Over the years I have come to recognise this presence as my guardian angel, my own personal Goddess. You could say my Goddess is a biker chick. I am not gifted with walking in the spiritual world like many other Pagans, but I know my pleas to my Goddess are often fulfilled and my questions usually answered. My Goddess is with me everywhere; at home and at work, she is there when I am out with friends and also when I am making love. Importantly she is there when my spirits are low and when I am in need.

I first asked for the help of the Goddess, wishing for strength, courage and protection in 2010 when I fought as the Holly King against the Oak King during a Summer Solstice ceremony at Stonehenge (see *Paganism 101* – Moon Books). The Goddess came good and I have come to trust in her ever since. She has not let me down yet.

I greet the world each morning from my doorstep that faces the rising sun. I welcome the Gods and Goddesses and Lords and Ladies of the East before reflecting on the importance of the element of Air. Next I call on the Lord of Plenty, the Dagda with his Cauldron of Abundance to sustain me throughout the coming day. During the day I always give the Goddess thanks for any good fortune that comes my way and project her love through me outwards into the world around me.

My Goddess has yet to reveal her name to me. I see her as a combination of the Earth Goddess, the Mother Goddess that resides in the heavens and the Goddess that connects my soul to the higher realms. She is the Goddess of St Andrews Ruin, a Cistercian-built church that nestles in a valley overlooking the English Channel. Now abandoned and decayed, the ruin is a place of magic and intrigue, an ideal place for both meditation and ritual. As a volunteer Coastal Ranger on Portland, I took it on myself to tidy up and manage the neglected overgrown ruin. Bramble and buddleia had invaded the space that was believed to have been a temple to the Goddess Venus in Roman times before a Saxon church was built in its place in the 7th century. The Cistercian monks completely rebuilt the church on the old foundations in 1148. St Andrews was destroyed by a landslip in 1759. I sense the Goddess watching as I work in the ruin and can feel her gratitude as she stirs from a long deep sleep.

I am a part of the Dolmen Grove, a Pagan group spread out over the south coast of England. The Grove is a spiritual minded group whose members include witches, Druids, shamans, pirates and Vikings, a family of likeminded souls who are allowed to be themselves without judgement or prejudice. We hold ceremonies and create spells to bring peace into the world and heal the hurt of the planet. The Portland and Weymouth moots regularly come together to hold ceremonies at the Circle of Stones in Tout Quarry to help ease the pain of the large amounts of stone extracted from the island, destroying the many Bronze Age stone circles and monuments that once covered Portland. The limestone is still being ripped out of the land and transported around the globe in the name of profit. There is still much work to do.

A Slow Journey Home

By Oakwood Leaf

For the past 30 years or so, the Christian Church has been a second home to me. Its seasons, rhythms and rituals have become part of who I am. The cycle of Harvest, Advent, Christmas, Lent and Easter – not to mention numerous other, smaller festivals – have marked out my year for decades. And now I earn my keep as a priest in the Church of England, called to help others to become part of that cycle, too.

But over the past three or four years, things have begun to change; much of what was once certain and familiar has become less so. The faith that had shaped my thinking and my understanding of the world began to feel inadequate and small – it no longer fitted the person I felt I now was.

For example, my Christian faith had very little to say about the body and how it is linked to the mind and spirit. And what it did say was, historically, largely negative. Nor did my faith seem to find room for expressions of the Divine Feminine – the language and imagery of the Church was almost exclusively male.

I also became increasingly saddened and frustrated that emotion, intuition and wisdom played no part in our worship, our learning or our way of relating to the world. Not only that, but as my own appreciation of nature grew stronger, I became increasingly bewildered by the way in which Christians claimed to worship the creator of the world and yet allowed no room for engagement with creation. I longed for a way to leave behind our church buildings (and our obsession with maintaining them!) and to seek God in nature.

Of course, given my role as a priest in the Church, these feelings and longings were not easy to acknowledge. Were these thoughts from God, or was I losing my faith? Was I failing in my duties as a faith-leader? If I allowed myself to pursue them would I be led away from the Church and all I had known over so many years?

And yet, at the same time, I knew in my heart that I was truly hearing a call: a call to open myself to new understandings; to explore new traditions; to journey, as a good friend and colleague put it, 'into the green'. Despite the struggles I felt inside, I knew that had to follow these new and strange paths.

The first step I took was an exploration of yoga – a practice that brought together for me the elements of body, mind and spirit. Some Christians told me that this activity would lead me away from Christ. Such comments failed to deter me; rather, I found that the beauty and stillness of yoga led me to discover new aspects of Christ as mystic, wise-man and teacher.

A little further along the path, I came into contact with a movement called Forest Church. Although its roots are in the Christian tradition, Forest Church groups are free to find their own way of working. The group to which I belong, and which I help to lead, wanders the fertile ground between the Celtic Christian tradition and Pagan paths. We celebrate the eight-fold year, we honour Christ and the Goddess and we gather for ritual in fields, gardens and woodland. We learn together, feast together, laugh together and help each other to walk the particular path that each person feels called to travel.

After several years of daring to walk this new path, my spirituality is a very varied landscape. I am still a priest, and continue to find it a privilege to serve the people of my Church. But now I pray both with words and by grounding myself into the earth. On my personal altar are a wooden cross, crystals, a hawthorn wand and images of the Christ-child and the Triple Goddess. On some days I feel brave and on others I feel like I am still only beginning. Mostly, though, I feel like I am slowly coming home.

Turtle Story: Between the Land, the Sea and the Sky

By Simon Wakefield

We have been walking for half an hour. Nothing definite yet, but in the distance the familiar faint line of a possible track has just come into view. The sea is flat calm, gently – almost imperceptibly – lapping on the cool sand. Another hour and the climbing sun will start to warm the beach for another day, sending heat deep enough to incubate the clutches of sea turtle eggs we have already found and protected with metal cages.

We work at the meeting point of land, sea and sky. The elements dominate. Sun, sand, sea...and quite often after 10 o'clock a strong wind that sends the sand grains tumbling and flying. We carry goggles to protect our eyes in case we get caught while we dig, one of many reasons why our morning beach walk starts at dawn.

We get closer. Yes, a female loggerhead has crawled up the beach during the night and, judging from the camouflage she has made, probably nested. I can't think of a stronger expression of the Wheel of the Year than the annual cycle of mating, nesting, incubation, hatching and struggle to the water of the hatchlings that we see on our Cretan beaches. No creature is as determined, as vulnerable, as a sea turtle hatchling making its first trip to the sea.

Walking the beach every morning during the summer, from the end of May to the beginning of October, is the way I can express so much of what I hold dear in the Druid path I have chosen. It makes a difference. More hatchlings reach the sea than would otherwise without our help. The beaches are used by both turtles and humans, but the protected nests are respected. If there are too many bright lights nearby at hatching time to exert their fatal attraction on hatchlings seeing the world for the first time, we build narrow corridors to bring them to the water's edge. Sometimes we move a newly laid nest out of harm's way if mama turtle has chosen a risky spot. Over the summer it all makes a big difference.

And it connects me, profoundly, with the cycle of life, and sometimes, death.

We start to locate the clutch. We patiently work through a well-rehearsed procedure and patiently probe the damp sand until the top of the nest chamber is located. Gently scraping back the topmost layer the last egg to be laid is just revealed, still glistening wet from the mother's juices. If you like to get your hands dirty for Lover Earth, for me this is about as good as it gets.

As a biologist and scientist I understand the ecological benefits for what we do, but at the same time question the dogmatic application of a rationalist-reductive view of life that empties the world of meaning. As T.S. Eliot asked: 'Where is the wisdom we have lost in knowledge?'

As a follower of a Druid path, which perceives the sacred in everything of this world, I am more inclined to the view Rilke expressed in the Ninth of his Duino Elegies (1923): 'Truly being here is so much; because everything here apparently needs us, this fleeting world, which in some strange way keeps calling us.'

The most profound experience of my life was to lie behind a nesting female loggerhead sea turtle on a starlit Greek beach. Putting aside all the requirements to measure and monitor I decided to just be present, and I opened up to an experience of deep time and an ancient longing by another creature simply to be, to express its uniqueness, which has never left me. For this reason I am doing what I do, working towards, as Charles Eisenstein would say: 'The more beautiful world our hearts know is possible.'

Finding Time for Paganism

By Sindy Leah Coumes Fitz

Following the Goddess in this modern age is a chore in itself. Fitting in the time to worship is a struggle, but if you leave this critical state of mind and spirituality to slip through your fingers because of work, children, housework etc, you are truly not giving yourself the opportunity for clarity, strength and growth.

I myself have five children, a husband, household and work. I manage to incorporate everything I need into simple everyday Pagan living. With one exception I celebrate holidays on a grand scale; as the Christians do Christmas my family celebrates the Winter Solstice/Yule. I have learned to combine all those popular holidays into our holidays. Having kids in school hearing about Santa and the Easter Bunny can make raising a Pagan child a little difficult and confusing. Give yourself some time to sit down and correlate the holidays, not because you need to but because in this day and age it is a part of society and it's not a cop out to do this. It allows you more freedom to express yourself and more tools to do so. I explain exactly what and why we celebrate and it also gives me the chance to teach my children religious differences and to be respectful of all beliefs. What a wonderful gift to give a child, an open educated mind.

Having had said this, indulge your Pagan side, invite your family and friends to participate in spellwork and rituals. Show them who you are and what you do instead of letting speculation get the better of them. Give them the gift of an open, educated mind. Navigate ways to use everyday spells with each other. Think of it as so common, do it so often that it does just that, it becomes a common everyday symbol of worship that gives you strength and clarity to any situation. As you cook, consecrate your salt and your water. Bless yourself when you are feeling upset. Cleanse your home with sage as you do your daily chores. No need to mumble incantations under your breath, speak loud and clear, you are a Pagan and it is your religious freedom to do so. Christians bless themselves with the sign of the cross, even shout 'Amen'. Let it become a part of you and a part of your family; what your friends see when they visit. There is no need to hide who you are and what you can accomplish.

Okay, now there are times when you need to have some moments to yourself to do some casting of spells and that can be even more of a challenge. I find that casting in groups is wonderful, but I do feel the need to connect to certain deities on a private basis from time to time. This will also benefit the solitary practitioner.

I have been working on a way to help you understand how to get spells done quickly. This is a very hectic time for everyone and if we all had time to run around naked and spend hours on ritual we would, but I don't and I know many who have this same problem. Some purists will disagree with me, but that leaves us with the question, is it better to practice an abridged version or none at all? I have had times in my life when life was getting in the way of my craft; not that I have any disrespect for the practice, but there are times when no craft work gets done at all for months. We have all been there. So here you go, just the basics to making a spell really work without out all the pomp and circumstance.

First things first, get a clear idea of what you need the spell for. Do this at night before bed when you have a few moments to think about exactly what it is you are requesting. Overnight you will have engaged that energy while you are sleeping. In the morning while you are brushing your teeth, for example, think of what you need to gather. All this dwelling on it adds energy to your spell. Take a few moments during the day while you are waiting at a red light or making your children dinner, packing lunches or folding laundry, to picture the ritual in your mind.

Cast the circle and call your elements. This is all being done in the Astral and will remain there for you until you are ready. Of course gather your basics: a candle, some herbs possibly, a crystal. All the gathering is part of the spell and in preparing, you grow the energy that you will need.

Now even if it took you a week to do just this much, when you are ready, the kids are tucked into bed and your significant other is watching TV, ask to not be disturbed for a few minutes. Slip away into your bedroom, kitchen, backyard or patio. Light your candle and call on the deity of your choice. Take a minute to access all that energy you have stored away just for this moment and state exactly what you need, stating it in the present tense as if it is already happening: 'My bills are paid', 'I am working my new job'...etc. Demand it as you charge your herbs and crystals. Take another moment to meditate, perhaps a minute or two. Visualise the closing of your circle, state to the deity and elements they are released and thank them, snuff your candle and gather the rest of your herbs. Bury them, even if just in a potted plant, and place your crystals in a safe place until your spell has come to pass, then bury the crystal. This is easier and still respectful, just a little more manageable with the time restraints we have.

Democracy in a Traditional Witchcraft Coven

By Breaca Aranwen of Albion

Having personally been a Pagan for 15-plus years, having been around the 'scene' for a few years now and having personally experienced many forms of Paganism – from Eclectic Solitary Wicca, through to 'Family'-based British Traditional Witchcraft and then onto coven-based Eclectic Witchcraft – one of the things I have come across several times is the problem of those within the Craft developing an ego that is out of proportion to their position. This is usually to the detriment of the group to which they belong. At times this has pushed me away from some of the groups I have belonged to, and has now led me to the point where I co-run a Coven with other democratically likeminded travellers upon the Crooked Path.

Our group, the Hearth of Albion Coven, was conceived from the beginning to have a very different structure to most other Covens – whether they be Wiccan with roles of High Priestess and High Priest, or more similarly styled Traditional Witchcraft groups with the roles of Lady, Magister, Man in Black, Maid, Watcher, etc. Instead of a hierarchy with its attendant potential egotistic problems we decided between the five founders that from day one we would run the Coven as a democracy.

This means that unlike other groups, where there are leaders who will normally take control and lead, we tend to share the lead role, different people write and lead our rituals, with everyone taking their fair turn, and sharing the workload. At one rite I may be leading, at the next I may be tending the fire or acting as nothing more than one of the celebrants, this not only allows us all the chance to experience the joys and pitfalls of being in a position of power, but also keeps us all well grounded and prevents a runaway ego from becoming a problem. It is also tremendously liberating as an individual, not having to always plan, write, lead and direct proceedings all the time means that you can really enjoy just being, which does relieve some of the stresses that can build up in life.

For us this lack of permanent leadership also means that all who are initiated within the Coven then have an equal say as to any decisions that are required. For most decisions we agree that a quorum of Coveners can make a majority decision, but for more important decisions, such as whether to allow someone to join, then all of us have to be in agreement and theoretically one person can then veto any decision.

In addition, everyone within the Coven is treated as an equal, even those who have not yet completed their training and as such have not been formally initiated into the Coven. Everyone is treated with respect. All of us are aligned and work together as a group well. This fosters a really engaged and aligned group mind, where all feel as though they own the Coven, which not only empowers the individuals, but also means that we all 'serve' the Coven and our fellows. I have never before seen commitment of the level that our ways have engendered!

It has been said that trying to organise and reach alignment within a group of Witches – all of whom are individually strong people with their own valid viewpoints and ideas – is akin to herding cats, it can be done, but not without the possibility of some serious harm occurring along the way. When the Coven is run as a democracy, then it becomes simple as there is no need to herd anyone. Once the alignment, respect and commitment are in place, it becomes a harmonious whole and definitely a place that is welcoming to all.

Pagan Parenting: Apples, Ancestors and Zombies

By Thea Prothero

Samhain, Nos Calan Gaeaf, or as it's more commonly known these days, Halloween, is the most well-known Celtic Pagan festival in the UK. It is the only one of our festivals when we get to actually celebrate, party and rejoice with our non-Pagan friends and the wider general population. This means a considerable amount to my daughter who, at 11, has begun to realise that her family are a little less than conventional. We grow about 50 per cent of our own food, I bake most of our bread, we try to shop sustainably, which usually means buying second-hand, I mend rather than throw away, especially clothing, and we spend a lot of time outside in nature – you get the picture. (I should add that we do own a TV!)

I have always been extremely conscious of how children in our society are exposed to religion from school age, if not before, and have deliberately steered away from this within my parenting, though without being negative or judgemental of other religions and paths that do. My primary motive is that my daughter should make her own decisions, and with her own free will. Conversely I have never hidden my faith from her, because I believe that honesty is one of the most important gifts a parent can give and I know that she is aware of how enriched I am by my spiritual practice. Since she has been old enough to make some of her own choices, (in her case at the age of nine or ten) she has attended my Grove and stood in circle, once even reading a story she composed about the Goddess Bridget. She enjoys singing Christmas carols at her school's church services with her friends, and has sat in meditation, after asking many gruelling and astute questions, with some Buddhist friends of ours. These have been her choices. Being able to celebrate openly, even blatantly at Halloween, has given her a real sense of status within her social peer group – her friends think our house is the coolest, most creepily decorated and her parties still warrant comparison as THE role model.

To me, Samhain is our biggest, most important festival, I would say of greater significance than Christmas, but I think my daughter would disagree, ('Santa might be listening!') We tend to throw caution to the wind and decorate our house in suitably ghoulish tackiness – cobwebs, bats, and green-faced witches in all dark corners, even having a Halloween tree – covered in small Jack-o-lanterns, made from orange skins, and purple tinsel. Our meals are suitably gory – eyeball jelly and blood custard after severed fingers and brains (sausages and mash). Some of her friends come over and they watch *Dracula*, or the *The Witches of Eastwick*, for example, while getting into character. Vampires, zombies combined with witches, green face paints with oodles of pretend blood and strange blue hair seem to be the (dis)order of the day. This year, although there is no party, her friends still consider it the only place to come. Of course, Halloween wouldn't be Halloween without trick or treating and we all set off around 7pm, when it's dark, cold and misty, returning an hour or so later with bags full of e-numbered sticky sweets and chocolate. This is exactly the same as most other families in the UK – a Pagan holiday to celebrate the (un)dead! Sure, in the West it is filled with overt commercialism, too many sweets and hyper-active kids…but, hang on…isn't that exactly the same as another Christian holiday in a couple of months?

Careful or we might become mainstream!

Of course I would be remiss if I didn't add the other side to our Samhain. We have a few apple trees on our allotment, and although most of them are quite small yet, we are very fortunate to have inherited a 30-year-old dessert tree. If we are lucky we may get a late apple harvest, usually around mid-October. These apples are as much symbols of Samhain as pumpkins, and hopefully will sustain us with their sweet crispiness for a couple of months hence. As we pick them this year, I remind my daughter of the ancient Celts, our spiritual ancestors, who would have been bringing down their cattle from their fields, and fetching in the last of their crops to sustain them through the winter months. It is a fitting reminder of our comparatively easy lives, and as I cut an apple in half sideways showing her the five-pointed star in the middle, a symbol of the apple's ancient sacredness, of how important they have always been to our people – a link and thread between our ancestors and us.

My altar is in quite a private place, and usually only visited by myself and sometimes my daughter, who has on occasion, helped to decorate it, and made helpful suggestions as to what to include. At Samhain we create a very public Ancestor Altar in our hallway, featuring photos of our deceased loved ones, and symbols for our distant ancestors. We light a candle for each person we remember, reciting their names and offer especially prepared food, and apples to honour them. The ritual of lighting the candles is done for three nights in silence and contemplation. We might also visit somewhere of significance, such as a graveyard, maybe a long barrow, or sacred site to offer flowers to the dead. This sombre half of our observance is equally important and significant as the first. To me, from a parenting point of view, it perfectly illustrates the balance between living and death, both part of life, and that our bloodlines flow in a continuous circle.

Samhain was the start of new Celtic year, both the old and new are celebrated together – remembering and reflecting on the past year, that our dead family members are important symbols of our attachment to the past and the land, or earth we live on. We also have hope for the coming year, for the return of the light, and future harvests. What's not to celebrate?

Community Philosophy

By Robert L Scott

Paganism philosophies, teachings, and Pagan people as a whole, have influenced my view of community. There are views of community that have both grown and expanded since my journey into Paganism, first of the Pagan community and then the community of the world at large.

Whenever I hear of or meet another Pagan, there are some immediate assumptions that we have more in common than differences. Whatever their specific path, their identity as Pagan builds bridges, and we have some common ground. Some of the terms might be different, but there are common beliefs about the nature of the sacred, and the sacredness of nature. Names may be different, but it is generally expected that we try to tune into the seasons. There is some expectation of ritual, with the understanding that the structure may be different, but at its core ritual is a spiritual process to connect, celebrate, and to cause change. Some differences are overlooked. Other differences are embraced as opportunities for learning and awareness. Diversity, in the Pagan perspective, does not have to be divisive.

The Pagan community has and can influence political and social views, the same as any other community. It does not do so by way of a bully pulpit, or hierarchical spokespeople, but by individual voices speaking out, teaching, providing information, and encouraging critical thinking.

At the time of this writing, it amazes me the online presence that the Pagan community has. I suspect that many people from my generation first discovered various Pagan paths, and researched them initially online.

Magazines are primarily community written and supported, such as Circle Magazine, the publication of Circle Sanctuary, as well as Witches and Pagans, as examples. They are written by the community and for the community.

Community takes many forms. Some people meet regularly in a coven, circle, grove or other organised group. There are festivals and conventions. Others simply get together as friends.

Overall, Pagan events tend to have a feeling of everyone being a participant, and not just an observer or attendee, compared to some religious traditions in my experience.

My spirituality teaches me a sense of interconnectedness of all.

My view of community at large, from global to neighbourhood, has become very open, and has been creating in me a desire to not only be more aware, but also to participate in events and activities. I am conscious of becoming an active part of it, because if I am going to be part of it by default, I might as well be an active part. An ongoing common Pagan ethic is that of personal accountability, and personal responsibility, for both action, and inaction.

The – big air quotes here – 'Pagan Community' is not perfect, but no community is. We owe it to ourselves to strive to improve it, self-monitor, and at avoid bashing individuals, groups, and the big 'C' Community.

I have seen and met many great people, groups, and been affected by them. It is my hope and vision that it will grow in quality and sense of connectedness. This is part of the reason why I choose to participate in the Pagan Planet anthology, to be an active part of the written voice of the Pagan community.

Living a Life of Contradictions

By JR

I have struggled to write this piece because I felt that I should be writing about the really big things that my Paganism draws me to do. By that I mean external things like environmental campaigning, protesting against fracking, getting involved in politics etc. Yet although I am on the fringe of these campaigns I cannot personally commit everything I have to these causes without getting myself too lost and angry. Discussing my passion for household recycling just seemed a little small scale and I am sure many non-Pagans are equally as dedicated.

So I am just talking from the heart about what I am currently wrestling with on my journey as I find, embrace and express who I really am. This is throwing up huge challenges and contradictions. I struggle with the tussle between the different sides of who I am, what I believe and what I see and experience around me. I find 'the world' or more accurately the society that humans have created a very difficult and battering place to exist. I have a huge desire to do 'something' about it, but what is that something and how can I, so small, achieve anything? This then leads to the desire to escape, to remove myself from something so big and insurmountable that I feel so insignificant. Then I go outside and find a quiet place in the world and stop. I find that connection, that connection that reminds me it is not my job to solve all the problems and reminds me that I want to be a part of this amazing world and delight in all the wonderful things it offers freely to us. This connection reminds me that it is my job to live to the best of my ability, shine my light the brightest I can, to take responsibility for myself and my actions and like the pebble dropped into the lake let the ripples I make radiate out.

One of the things I do to help myself remain connected is to minimise my exposure to the media and advertising, which can be extremely difficult as it is all pervading. These like very much to tell you who you should be, how you should behave, what you should think, even down to how you should smell – to be acceptable. They like to keep us all small, scared and quiet. So I have stopped watching the news, I try to refrain from reading newspapers (except the good deed feed, which is always a great pick-me-up) and avoid getting drawn into discussions online, where sadly people get a kick out of confrontation for confrontation's sake. Yet on the flip side, by removing the media from my life I feel a little like I have copped out, that if I were just stronger I could remain fully connected to this world and retain my inner sense of self and ethics. This then can slip into recrimination turned inwards at my lack.

So part of my journey is about accepting who I am and what I need to do, to shine the brightest I can be. I strive every day to stand in my power, I revel in my childlike joy, let my enthusiasm, passion and laughter ooze out and infect others. So for now I cannot stand up at a protest, shout about what I think and feel when the prevailing thought is so opposite, all pervading and difficult to challenge. Instead I take responsibility for myself, practice self-care, and support those who can and do stand up for our planet against those who think it is theirs to abuse. So I take to my board and ride my wave of contradictions, this is my believing, belonging and being, well for the time being anyway.

Turning Earthwards

By Nimue Brown

When I first came to the Pagan community, nearly 20 years ago, it was often a very private, introspective sort of place. With fewer legal protections and less social acceptance, Pagans tended to be secretive. Beyond that, practice was often about the self, and a personal relationship with the natural world, and perhaps the gods of the natural world and the gods of our ancient ancestors. We'd turn up for a litter pick at Earth Day, but that was about it.

Since then, Paganism has become more public facing, in part because society has become more accepting of us. The more we educate people, the more acceptance there is – and that's a journey we can all be proud of. However, at the same time our collective consciousness has changed. You can't be a Pagan without having some environmental awareness. The past 20 years have brought increasingly painful revelations about the devastating impact humans are having on the planet, and the urgent need for change. The context for Paganism has shifted in my lifetime, because the Earth needs us. Private practice is no longer enough. In response, many of us become active, and activists. Our work becomes more focused on the need for change in this place, and these cultures. We are in the world, on behalf of the world.

I came into the Pagan Planet project late, having been asked to take on the editing. It is the sort of work I love – supporting and enabling other people in their creativity. That too is about taking Paganism into the world. Talking to contributors, I've seen the breadth and diversity of how people are manifesting their spiritual lives. The call to action is clear, and it comes in many ways. The call to make lifestyle changes, to live sustainably. The call to community, to politics, activism, and radical reimagining.

The call to care, to nurture, to protect. We turn to face the world, and we find our Pagan faiths guide us to certain ways of acting and being, certain needs we must answer. Each of us is called differently, and each of those callings matter.

Some callings are dramatic, taking a Pagan into frontline action and public scrutiny. Some callings are subtle, and all about how we interact with our most immediate and intimate tribes. All of these things make a difference. There is always more to be done than there is the means to undertake it. There is more to be dreamed, and there are better ways to be found. I hope that these diverse insights into what it means to live your faith will be an inspiration to others, and an affirmation. Whatever you are doing, to live your Paganism, it is good work, and part of something bigger and vitally important.

There is power in community. We are sustained by connections with likeminded people. Aware of other people's struggles and triumphs, we are reassured about our own ups and downs, and occasionally blessed with something to celebrate. Just knowing you aren't alone can be a powerful aid to keeping going. Seeing what others do can be profoundly inspiring. We are all simply people. Anyone can step up, to some kind of meaningful action. Anyone can find a place where their contribution is needed. Reach out a hand to someone else. Offer them a word of support. Share the story of your efforts and visions. Become part of creating something better.

It's tough out there right now. Activists get their hearts broken – repeatedly. I've come out of political fights bruised and exhausted. Sometimes I step forward, sometimes I have no choice but to step back and it is the same for all of us. It is painful to live with awareness of much that is wrong in the world. The more you know, the more it will hurt you and the more powerless you will feel. Without that heartbreaking knowledge, there is no scope to make change. We have a spiritual duty to know what humanity does, and a spiritual imperative to try and put that right.

Alongside this, are amazing opportunities for community and experience. I find great inspiration from the tribe that gathers every year at Druid Camp. I've made baby steps towards the Transition movement, and am doing a bit of gardening with a local project called Down to Earth Stroud. I help out in small ways with a local environmental charity, too. In these things I find joy, inspiration and camaraderie. I find reasons to be hopeful about the future.

Helping people do good stuff has been at the heart of my service as a Druid for a long time. That can manifest as making safe spaces where people can find their voices, and sing. I pile in when people need support to get their ideas further afield, an unofficial ethical marketing department for anything I chance upon that has no way of affording a marketing department. I share my stories via my blog, reaching out to other people who walk similar paths. There is some comfort in not being alone, and if I can offer that comfort by sharing, this is good. Often these are very small gestures set against the bigger picture, but I remind myself, and anyone else who anguishes over not doing enough, that the tides of history depend on amassing a lot of small actions. Grass roots change is what always makes the difference in the end. As a Pagan, I am very comfortable with the idea of being the grass roots.

Change hurts. Knowing hurts. There are days when I have to say no, when I cannot bear to learn anything more about rainforest devastation, of species loss, or the latest madness to fall from the lips of politicians. Staying open enough to keep caring without being broken by it is an ongoing challenge, and we all need to face it. In these difficult times, we need our bards and storytellers like never before, to remind us of how much better things could be, and to keep us hopeful. We need our artists to envisage better worlds. We need our warriors to show us how to keep standing up when all we want to do is crawl away, close our eyes and shove our fingers into our ears. We need our moots, covens, camps, hearths and groves as places of sanctuary and healing, where we can grieve, and celebrate, and find strength. We need to believe in each other, and build networks of support across our communities. We need to be sharing experience and energy, and we need to be kind to each other and take care of each other as much as we possibly can.

Because it comes down to this: we need this planet. It is our home. Where else do we belong, but here? It is all the future we have. It is our life, and our faith, and all that we hold sacred. We have a lot of work to do, as a consequence. Step up, be inspired, be willing to cry, and dance, and march and tell stories. This is an age that calls for courage, for vision and heroism, and we have the stories of our ancestors to help us find the means to do all those things.

MOON BOOKS

Moon Books invites you to begin or deepen your encounter with Paganism, in all its rich, creative, flourishing forms.